Coaching Wide Receiver Play

Matt Troxel

ISBN: 978-1-60679-247-6
Library of Congress Control Number: 2012955398
Cover design: Cheery Sugabo
Book layout: Studio J Art & Design
Front cover photo: ©David Hood/Cal Sport Media/ZUMAPRESS.com

Coaches Choice
P.O. Box 1828
Monterey, CA 93942
www.coacheschoice.com

Dedication

I want to dedicate this book to my wife Katie. Every time I thought I wouldn't be able to finish this book, you pushed me and reminded me I could do it. Your words of encouragement gave me the inspiration to finish this project. I don't know what I'd do without you.

Acknowledgments

I would like to thank Steve Axman for getting me to undertake this project and pushing me to finish. Without Ax, I would have never believed I could actually write or finish this book. I would also like to thank my parents, Van and Karen Troxel, for supporting me over the years no matter what the situation or project was. Most of what I know about coaching I've learned from them.

Contents

Introduction

Coaching Wide Receiver Play is a complete and thorough book to help you, the coach, produce effective and efficient wide receiver play for your offense. Playing wide receiver is one of the most—if not *the* most—unique positions on the football field. No other offensive or defensive position gets to achieve the variety of tasks during a game that a wide receiver does. Wide receivers get to catch the football, run with the football, run pass routes, score touchdowns, block, and sometimes even throw a pass. This book will provide you, the coach, with all the basic fundamentals and techniques that are required to coach effective and efficient wide receiver play for your team.

Coaching Wide Receiver Play can help you teach and coach the intricacies of the wide receiver position. This book will also help coaches at all levels of football understand how to properly coach wide receiver techniques and fundamentals. It offers step-by-step instruction on all aspects of playing the wide receiver position, and it features chapters on what attributes make up an effective wide receiver, stances and starts, catching, pass route running, releases, blocking, making plays after the catch, and recognizing coverages. Each chapter also includes drills that are designed to improve the skills and fundamentals of each topic covered in this all-inclusive book.

A wide variety of aspects to playing the wide receiver position, such as understanding how to read the opponent's defense, can often be overlooked. Whether you're a beginning coach or a veteran, *Coaching Wide Receiver Play* will help you to get your wide receivers to perform the multitude of tasks that can pop up during the course of a game. From pass route running to blocking, you, the coach, should understand how to properly teach basic fundamentals and techniques to the wide receiver position group. A wide receiver can rarely be great if he doesn't receive great coaching. This book will become for you, the coach, a basic blueprint on how to properly teach wide receiver techniques and fundamentals to all age groups and levels of experience. Likewise, you'll be able to understand the techniques and fundamentals it takes for a wide receiver to become an effective and efficient player.

1

Attributes of an Effective Wide Receiver

Before coaches learn about the technical aspects of creating effective and efficient wide receiver play, they should first understand the characteristics that make up an effective wide receiver. The wide receiver position is unlike any position on the football field. Throughout a football game, wide receivers have the opportunity to accomplish several tasks, including:

- Catching the football
- Running for extra yards
- Scoring touchdowns
- Blocking defenders during run plays
- Running the football in specially designed plays

Being able to accomplish all these different tasks throughout a football game makes the wide receiver position an extremely versatile position to play. This versatility accommodates the skills of a variety of different athletes, making it one of the most appealing positions to play in all of football.

The flexibility needed to play wide receiver is a reason why so many different types of athletes can play the position. Effective wide receivers have come in many different sizes, speeds, shapes, and forms. Offenses have had big physical wide receivers who create huge targets for the quarterback; tall wide receivers who are great at jumping up, over, and around defensive backs to make catches; small wide receivers who use great quickness to create big plays with their running ability after they catch the football;

and other wide receivers who lack great speed but become expert pass route runners to gain separation from a defensive back to make catches. Still other wide receivers possess blazing speed that gives an offense the ability to stretch a defense vertically and horizontally. The truly great receivers possess many—if not all—of these physical attributes. Some very fine wide receivers possess a number of these qualities and attributes but not all of them. For a player to become an efficient wide receiver, he should maximize the talents he does have and do whatever he can to improve the skills he doesn't seem to naturally possess.

Confidence at the Wide Receiver Position

The number one attribute it takes to become an effective wide receiver is confidence. A wide receiver should have supreme confidence in the abilities he has if he's going to be successful. If he doesn't believe he's going to make the big catch or make the big play, then he probably won't become an effective and efficient wide receiver. The wide receiver position is designed specifically for athletes who believe they have what it takes to become a great player. Without confidence, a wide receiver can't ever expect to accomplish the variety of tasks asked of him throughout the course of a football game. A confident wide receiver should believe that the defensive back assigned to cover him can't get the job done. A confident wide receiver believes that when the ball is in the air, the football is his ball, not the defender's. A confident wide receiver believes on third down that the ball should be thrown to him because he knows he's the one who's going to make the first-down catch. At all times, wide receivers should believe they have what it takes to accomplish the task at hand. As soon as he takes the field for pre-game warm-ups, a wide receiver should think he's the best player on the field. He should believe that when the football is snapped, no one can stop him.

To develop confidence in his abilities, a wide receiver should firmly believe he's great and then strive to maintain this belief. To gain the confidence needed to be successful, a wide receiver should try to stay positive at all times. The fastest way to lose confidence is through negative self-talk. If a wide receiver drops the football, the worst thing he can do is doubt his ability to catch the football. Instead, a wide receiver should try to develop the "next play" attitude. The next play attitude is used to encourage positive thoughts for the next play and is used after a player has just experienced a negative production play. As soon as a negative play is over, a wide receiver should be coached to think positively to get his mind ready for the next play. If a wide receiver drops a pass, the first thought that should go through his head is that the next time the football is thrown his way, he's going to catch it. Developing the next play attitude and positive thinking are crucial to becoming an effective wide receiver. Negative thoughts, such as saying "I can't catch" or "I'm not fast enough," reinforce to a wide receiver that he's not capable of performing his assigned task. Over time, negative thoughts and self-talk can lead a wide receiver to put a mental block in the way of his abilities. Positive thoughts and self-talk should be encouraged at all times. With positive thinking, a wide receiver can develop the confidence needed to be an effective wide receiver.

To help develop confidence in his wide receivers, the wide receivers coach needs to work to create a constant confident attitude that every wide receiver can believe in. An attitude of believing they can execute the skills being taught and coached is essential to developing confident wide receivers. A wide receiver coach can help this process by making corrections seem easy, such as: "You're taking your eyes off the ball at the last second. Just look the ball all the way into your hands." Making corrections seem easy will develop confidence within the whole position group compared with being negative, which will reinforce negative thoughts among players.

Competiveness and Effort at the Wide Receiver Position

Wide receivers need to be the most competitive athletes on the football field. When the football is thrown, a wide receiver should have a burning desire to battle for the football from a defender to make the catch. When a football game is hanging in the balance in the fourth quarter with the score tied, a competitive wide receiver will want the ball thrown to him. A wide receiver can be very confident in his abilities on the football field, but if he doesn't like to compete, he won't be able to showcase the confidence he's developed in his abilities.

To become a great competitor, a wide receiver should hate failure and have a burning hunger for success. The fear of failure is a thought that should drive a wide receiver to be successful. Fear of failure shouldn't drive a wide receiver to think negatively about an upcoming play. Instead, the fear of failure should be used to motivate a wide receiver to dig deeper and compete fiercely to help his team achieve victory.

To develop into a great competitor, a wide receiver should give maximum effort in all the game's phases. A competitive wide receiver practices at game day speed with game day effort at all times. In the off-season, a competitive wide receiver will spend the extra time needed to become a better football player, improving day to day. Wide receivers should give maximum effort in the weight room, getting bigger and stronger for the upcoming season. They need to spend time by themselves working on individual techniques that will make them a better wide receiver in all facets of their game. True competitors strive to outwork their opponents and will expend the extra effort needed to accomplish their lofty goals.

Toughness at the Wide Receiver Position

If a wide receiver plays with confidence and maximum effort and likes to compete, then developing toughness shouldn't be a problem. Being mentally and physically tough is an attribute every wide receiver should strive to achieve. To accomplish this task, a wide receiver should be ready to sacrifice his own body for his team. If a wide receiver is going up to catch a slant route over the defense's middle, he should be willing to absorb a crushing hit from a safety to achieve the desired goal of catching the pass. The willingness to sacrifice his body for the good of the team displays the amount of toughness it takes to become an effective wide receiver.

The wide receiver position isn't known for having the toughest and most physically imposing players on the field. Wide receivers are often characterized as pretty boys, prima donnas, or for being soft. These images and attitudes are stereotypes that have no place in effective wide receiver play. It's imperative to change these stereotypes. To make such a change, coaches should encourage and reward toughness and physical play. Wide receivers can't be allowed to shy away from contact if the desired level of toughness on the field is going to be achieved. Wide receivers should learn how to play physically tough football. This can be done through extra emphasis on run blocking and catching the ball over the defense's middle or not running out-of-bounds at the end of a run. Taking steps to emphasize tough, physical play in practice will carry over to the game field. A wide receiver can't be expected to be a tough physical player if he isn't required to be the type of tough, physical player on the practice field every day.

Along with being a tough physical player, a wide receiver should strive to be equally mentally tough. Dealing with adversity and adjusting to setbacks during practices and games can be a difficult task for a wide receiver to accomplish. The mentally tough wide receiver will use the next play attitude he's developed to turn adverse situations into positive ones. The mentally tough wide receiver doesn't let the crowd or an opponent deter him from accomplishing his assigned task. Instead, when facing adverse conditions, the mentally tough wide receiver puts greater emphasis on his assignment. Mental toughness can be developed by pushing a wide receiver to his physical limits and maybe even beyond. The mentally tough wide receiver should be able to think even though he's tired and still be able to execute his assignment. Even when his body is saying he can't play anymore, the mentally tough wide receiver should learn to play through physical discomfort and have his mind clear to execute his assignment. Becoming a mentally and physically tough wide receiver is an essential characteristic to becoming an effective wide receiver.

Concentration at the Wide Receiver Position

An effective wide receiver should have exceptional focus and concentration. When the football is in the air, a wide receiver should have the ability to block out everything around him and concentrate on catching the football. A wide receiver shouldn't be distracted by the crowd or the defender covering him. Even when a wide receiver knows he's going to take a big hit from a defender, his focus and concentration should never be altered from tracking the football all the way to his hands and then securely tucking the football away under his armpit. An effective wide receiver concentrates and focuses on the football from the moment it leaves the quarterback's hand to the moment the football comes into the grasp of his hands. Developing great focus and concentration is a must to becoming an effective wide receiver when the football is in the air.

Having great awareness of himself and his surroundings is another aspect of concentration and focus an effective wide receiver should possess. In the pass game, wide receivers run many different pass routes. Some pass routes are run off a certain number of steps taken by a wide receiver; an example would be a seven-step post route. Some routes require a wide receiver to reach a certain depth on the field before he can break his route off, such as a 15-yard dig route. All these different route variations require a wide receiver to have great awareness of his body and of where he is in regard to his positioning on the field. A wide receiver should be able to count the number of steps he's taking while at full speed to run certain pass routes correctly. The same can be said if a wide receiver is running a pass route to a certain depth on the football field. A wide receiver should be aware of landmarks on the football field, which can tell him at what point he should break his route off.

The boundaries on the football field, the down and distance markers, and the time on the game clock are other aspects of a football game a wide receiver should constantly be aware of. Being aware of where the sideline is can be the difference between a completion and an incompletion. A wide receiver should know where the sideline is to ensure he can get one foot in bounds if he's making a sideline catch. If a wide receiver's landmark is the front pylon of the end zone for a comeback out route, he should be aware of where the front pylon is relative to the breakpoint of his pass route. This will ensure his body is within the end zone at the moment he catches the ball to score a touchdown.

At all times, a wide receiver should be aware of what down it is and how many yards his team needs to gain a first down. Before every play, a wide receiver should look at the yard and down markers to ensure he's aware of how many yards he needs for a first down. Knowing the down and distance situation will help a wide receiver make sure he runs his routes to the proper depth. If a wide receiver is running a six-yard hitch route and its third down and six yards to go, a wide receiver should be sure to run his hitch route a full seven yards to ensure he gains a first down for his team. Finally, a wide receiver should always know how much time is left on the game clock. If only 30 seconds to play remain and a wide receiver catches a pass near the sideline, he needs to know he should try to step out-of-bounds to stop the game clock. Being aware of how much time is left on the clock can be the difference between a win or a loss.

Developing great field and defensive positioning awareness will allow a wide receiver to understand what type of scheme a defense is preparing to run. Before the snap of every play, an effective wide receiver should be aware of what the defensive pre-snap alignment is. Analyzing the defensive alignment before the snap can be tremendously helpful to understanding what scheme a defense will run on the upcoming play. Being aware of his football surroundings allows a wide receiver to focus more on the task at hand. It will allow him to concentrate on his individual assignment and block out any potential distractions around him to become a more effective player.

Being a Selfless Wide Receiver

A key attribute to becoming an effective wide receiver is learning to become a selfless football player. The wide receiver position is at times known for being a selfish position. Wide receivers have the reputation of not wanting to block or only running pass routes full speed when they know they're getting the football. For a wide receiver to truly be effective, he needs to develop a team-first attitude and truly become a selfless football player. Many times throughout a football game, a wide receiver should run a pass route that's used to get another wide receiver open. A slot receiver can be asked to run a vertical streak route to clear out a safety for a dig route that's being run underneath a streak route by his teammate. The slot receiver should realize that his streak route is the key route and should be run at full speed. By running the streak route with great speed and intensity, the slot receiver will open up the dig route for his teammate to make a catch for a big gain. This type of selfless play is what wins games. To develop this type of selfless play attitude, a wide receiver should be willing to give up individual glory for the benefit of his team. A wide receiver should block on run plays with the same effort and intensity he puts into his pass routes. A selfless wide receiver should never be driven by a fear of competition or a fear of failure. He should be driven by the fear of letting his teammates down. If this type of fear has been reached, then a wide receiver has developed a healthy fear, which is essential to becoming a selfless player and an effective wide receiver.

Body Control at the Wide Receiver Position

Great wide receivers have excellent control over their bodies throughout every play. Developing great body control is an essential element to becoming an effective wide receiver. A wide receiver should be able to contort and move his body in many different directions and angles throughout the course of a football game. Having great body control will allow a wide receiver to run in direction and reach behind himself in the opposite direction to catch a pass that's thrown behind his body. A wide receiver should be able to go from full speed to a dead stop in a second's notice to escape a defender's grasp. Without great body control, this task can be very difficult. Great body control will allow an effective wide receiver to react to sudden changes during the flight of a pass or to be able to tiptoe the sideline after a pass is caught to gain extra yardage. Great body control allows a wide receiver to absorb a crushing hit by a defender and still come up with a catch. An effective wide receiver will strive to understand and develop his body control to become an effective wide receiver.

Speed at the Wide Receiver Position

An effective wide receiver ideally possesses great speed. Having great speed allows a wide receiver to stretch the defense vertically and horizontally. A wide receiver with great speed can run by defenders in the vertical pass game, which will create big plays for the offense. Having great speed will also allow a wide receiver to run away from defenders once he has the ball in his hands. A wide receiver can make up for other shortcomings in his attributes if he has great speed. If a wide receiver is a poor route runner, his speed can often compensate for his inability to run precise routes. This type of wide receiver can be used to run such vertical routes as a streak or post route to best utilize his speed. Having great speed could make a poor route runner a valuable asset to a team. No matter what a wide receiver's skill set is, if a wide receiver has great speed, a defender should always respect the fact a speed wide receiver can beat him vertically for a big play. Having great speed is by no means the defining characteristic of an effective wide receiver. Many other attributes covered in this book will help make an effective wide receiver. Having great speed is a very effective attribute to have. However, a wide receiver can make up for a lack of speed by developing and refining other areas. That being said, speed is an attribute a wide receiver can never have enough of and should always be an area a wide receiver is looking to improve.

Quickness at the Wide Receiver Position

An effective attribute that can offset a wide receiver's lack of speed is having great quickness. Quickness is the ability to move in absence of a lot of external force and without any windup. This means that if a wide receiver is running a streak route, a quick wide receiver will take less time to get to full speed than a wide receiver who lacks such quickness. This doesn't mean the quick wide receiver is faster than the wide receiver who lacks quickness; it only means it takes less time for the quick wide receiver to reach his individual top speed.

Quickness can also be another word for explosiveness or reaction time. A quick wide receiver takes less time to react to a defender's movement than a wide receiver who's lacking quickness. Quick wide receivers usually have an innate ability to make defenders miss tackles, which makes a quick wide receiver an ideal candidate to have plays designed for him to run with the football. Quicker wide receivers are also better candidates to be inside slot receivers. Slot receivers have to navigate through more defenders because their alignments are closer to the football. Having a quick slot receiver can make this process easier to manage.

Having great quickness will also allow a wide receiver to run more efficient pass routes. A quick wide receiver is usually better at running such precision routes as a dig route or a comeback out route than a wide receiver who lacks quickness. Great quickness also gives a wide receiver a better chance to beat a defender who's playing press coverage against him. Being quick will allow a wide receiver to anticipate a press defender's movement at the snap of the ball and move the opposite way to gain a release. For a wide receiver to be an effective player, developing his quickness to his best degree is essential.

Size and Strength at the Wide Receiver Position

If a wide receiver doesn't possess great quickness, a way to deal with this inefficiency is to have either size or great strength—if not both. Big wide receivers can make up for their lack of quickness with their size. A big wide receiver offers a huge target for the quarterback to throw to. A big wide receiver can use his body and size to gain an advantageous position against a defender to catch the football. Big wide receivers create match-up problems for defenses to consider. The average defensive back is 5'10" and often smaller than that. If a 6'4" wide receiver lines up against a 5'10" defensive back, the match-up should favor the 6'4" wide receiver. Having big targets to throw to makes the quarterback's job easier. A quarterback can be less accurate with big wide receivers because of their size. He can take more chances by throwing a jump ball to the big wide receiver, which utilizes a big wide receiver's size advantage over a defensive back who's shorter.

Having big strong wide receivers is a great luxury to have when developing an offensive game plan. Like the other attributes mentioned, size or strength offers another way to offset an attribute a wide receiver might not possess. It's not essential for a wide receiver to have great size. Many great wide receivers throughout history haven't been very big. When a wide receiver lacks size, having great strength is all the more important. A small wide receiver should make up for his lack of size with strength or quickness. Whether a wide receiver is big or small, the key is to offset his physical limitations with other attributes and intangibles that can still make him a complete and effective wide receiver.

2

Wide Receiver Catching Fundamentals

When a coach asks a wide receiver what his job is, the answer should include "to catch the ball." A wide receiver has three main jobs: to block, to run, and to catch. This chapter will focus on catching the football. Catching the football is a basic fundamental of football but can be one of the hardest things in football to accomplish. Many factors influence whether a wide receiver gets the chance to catch the ball. The offensive line should protect the quarterback long enough for the football to be delivered. The quarterback should deliver a precisely thrown pass to a wide receiver. A wide receiver should run an excellent pass route and be in position to catch the ball. If all these tasks are accomplished during a play, then a wide receiver should catch and maintain possession of the football.

Learning to catch the football is a process that takes time and effort. Catching is a skill not all people have. With the right amount of hard work and effort, a wide receiver can become a better pass catcher. To be a great pass catcher, a wide receiver should spend time catching and handling the football on a daily basis. Even at home, a wide receiver can grab a friend and go play catch in the front yard or on the practice field. When a wide receiver is lying in bed, he can throw a ball up in the air and practice catching it. Wide receivers don't always need a football to become good at catching. Bouncing and catching a tennis ball or a racquetball off a wall is a great way to practice catching. Little tricks like these will pay off on the football field. Developing great hand-eye coordination will cause a wide receiver to catch more footballs on the field and become a better all around football player.

Multiple types of catches can be performed on the football field, including the shoulder-level catch, the over-the-shoulder catch, the below-the-waist catch, the behind-the-body catch, the pocket catch, the one-handed catch, and the sideline catch. All these different catches are used at different times throughout a game. Each different type of catch has a different skill and technique that should be mastered to perform the catch on a consistent basis. Before wide receivers learn about these different types of catches, coaches should help them understand the basic fundamentals of catching the football.

Catching Fundamentals

Catching the football is an intricate process that involves multiple body parts. The eyes should be concentrated and focused on the football. The arms should be outstretched and attack the football. The hands need to be relaxed and soft, and the legs and body should be ready to twist and bend toward the football's flight. All the different limbs of a wide receiver's body should be able to act in perfect unison to catch the football. It's important to remember that this process is called *catching*, but what a wide receiver is actually doing is receiving the football from the quarterback and delivering it to a secure tucked position until the play is over. A wide receiver doesn't want to fight the football with his hands; he wants to absorb the football into his hands and deliver the football to a tucked position in his body.

Eye Placement Fundamentals

The number one thing a wide receiver should possess to catch the football is to have great concentration. A wide receiver's eyes should be able to track the football from the moment it leaves the quarterback's hand to the moment it hits a wide receiver's hands and is safely tucked away. From the moment the football leaves the quarterbacks hands, a wide receiver should find a spot on the football and concentrate on that area. A common way to teach a wide receiver to find a concentration spot is to make the football's white stripe the concentration spot. The white stripe is a great place for a wide receiver to focus his eyes during the football's flight. The white stripe creates a color contrast from the brown football, which makes the white stripe an ideal concentration spot for a wide receiver to use. Another great concentration spot is the football's front tip. The front tip creates a crosshair where the four seams of a football come together and serves as a great spot for a wide receiver to focus his eyes on during the football's flight. Each different wide receiver over time will develop a concentration spot that works best for his individual needs. The concentration spot can be left up to the individual wide receiver and what works best for him. Coaches should make sure each wide receiver has a concentration spot and that he understands why he should have a place to concentrate his eyes. Having a concentration spot for the eyes to focus on is the key to tracking the football during its flight path.

The last three yards of the football's flight path into a wide receiver's hands is the most crucial part for a wide receiver's eyes. During this stage, a wide receiver's eyes should be totally focused on the football and nothing else. The last three yards of the football's flight path is when wide receivers tend to take their eyes off the ball in preparation to run after the catch. It's critical for a wide receiver to have complete concentration during the last three yards of the football's flight path and to watch the football hit his hands and then be tucked safely away. The eyes should be positioned behind the hands at the point where the ball hits a wide receiver's hands. A wide receiver's eyes should be focused on his concentration spot and stay focused on that spot throughout the tuck process. During the tuck, a wide receiver's eyes should stay focused on the football.

The tuck process is another area where wide receivers tend to take their eyes off the football. Taking his eyes off the football can cause a wide receiver to drop the football or not securely tuck the football properly. During the flight path, if total focus on the concentration spot is reached, the ball can seem to be moving in slow motion for a wide receiver. This sense of heightened concentration is something every wide receiver should strive to accomplish but can only be achieved if a wide receiver properly understands where to focus his eyes during the football's flight path.

Arms and Hands Catching Fundamentals

During the process of catching the football, a wide receiver should make his hands as big as possible. He should spread his fingers apart to increase the surface area where the ball can successfully land. The basic blueprint for how the football should be caught is for a wide receiver to form a noose with his hands around the football. The thumbs and index fingers should be touching, creating a noose around the football. The fingers are spread and ready to tighten the noose around the football. The football should always be caught with the fingertips, not the palms. As the football enters a wide receiver's hands, his fingers should squeeze around the ball, tightening his noose on the football. A wide receiver's hands should remain relaxed upon the football's impact.

It's imperative that a wide receiver remembers he's not catching the football—he's receiving the football. No wide receiver should ever have tight, stiff fingers when attempting to catch the football. Instead, the fingers and hands remain relaxed and soft. Stiff fingers and hands make it difficult for a wide receiver to successfully catch the football with his fingertips. Relaxed hands by a wide receiver create the notion of receiving or absorbing the football into a tucked secure position. Stiff fingers and hands will give off the notion to a wide receiver's body that he's trying to fight the football or bring it to a dead stop. Having stiff hands and fingers will cause the football to bounce off a wide receiver's hands instead of being absorbed into his hands. If a wide receiver's hands stay relaxed, then so will his arms, which makes the process of catching the football more likely to be successful for a wide receiver.

When a wide receiver attempts to catch the football, his arms and hands should be able to extend from his body in a split second. During a pass route, it's imperative for a wide receiver to keep his elbows bent at a 90-degree angle and to execute great running form. His arms and elbows should never be below waist level during a route. His arms need to remain tight to the body and be ready to attack the football at any moment. If a wide receiver runs with poor form, with the elbows not bent at 90 degrees and with the arms below waist level, it can be hard for a wide receiver to get his arms up in time to catch a high pass. If a wide receiver's arms are tight to the body and high, they'll always be in the right position to catch the football. When attempting to catch the football, a wide receiver should always remember to attack the football with his arms and hands. A wide receiver's arms should extend from his body toward the football. A wide receiver doesn't want to catch the football with his body. Instead, a wide receiver wants to catch the football with his hands. His elbows act as shock absorbers when the football is delivered from the air to a secure tucked position by his hands.

Body Control Fundamentals

It's important to remember that a wide receiver's body isn't used to catch the football. Instead, his body is used to position his arms and hands to catch the football. A wide receiver's body should be able to move in one synchronized motion with his hands to catch the football. During a catch, a wide receiver's body should remain relaxed and be ready to move and be contorted at all sorts of different angles for his hands to catch the football. The primary function of a wide receiver's body is to act as shield between the defensive back and the football. For a successful catch to occur, a wide receiver should use his body to keep the defender away from the football's flight. A wide receiver's body should be positioned in front of the football and between a defender for a successful catch to occur. As the football approaches a wide receiver, the upper torso and the head should keep still, ensuring the body is relaxed in preparation to catch the football. If a wide receiver successfully relaxes his torso, then the body will be ready to softly cushion the catching of the football.

Shoulder-Level and
Above-the-Head Catching Techniques

Catching the football at shoulder level and above the head involves using the noose catch technique mentioned earlier. The noose catch technique is shown in Figure 2-1. When using the noose catch technique to catch footballs thrown above a wide receiver's head or at shoulder level, a wide receiver should make his hands as big as possible in order to create as much surface area as he can for the hands to absorb the football. A wide receiver's fingers are spread apart as wide as possible. While working to spread his fingers, a wide receiver should remember to keep his fingers and hands relaxed throughout the noose catch. The thumbs and index fingers are pointed inward at each other. The inward-facing thumbs and index fingers create a noose, which will be used

Figure 2-1. This figure shows the proper way to catch a football thrown at shoulder level or above. The thumbs are pointing inward at each other. The index fingers are also pointing inward at each other.

by a wide receiver to strangle and tighten around the football as the ball enters a wide receiver's fingertips. When using the noose catch technique, a wide receiver should always remember to extend his arms at the football as it enters his hands. Extending his arms at the football is especially important when a wide receiver is attempting to catch the football thrown over his head. The extended arms are a good way for a wide receiver to sight the football's flight with his eyes into his hands.

Below-the-Waist Catching Techniques

For a wide receiver to properly catch a football that's thrown below his waist, he should use the pinkies in, thumbs out catching technique (Figure 2-2). When a football is thrown below his waist, a wide receiver should prepare to flip his hands over and perform the pinkies in, thumbs out catch. A wide receiver's hands should flip over so the back of his hands are facing the ground. His pinkies are touching each other facing inward and his thumbs are facing out. The elbows need to be brought in tight to the body, which will enable the pinkies to touch each other. If the elbows are flared out, then a wide receiver's pinkie fingers can't assume the proper position. A wide receiver also needs to make sure his thumbs are hyperextended outward so the thumbs don't interfere with the catching process. If a wide receiver's thumbs are bent inward across the palm, the wide receiver won't be able to properly perform a below-the-waist catch. If a wide receiver's hands and elbows are positioned properly, then a scoop or basket should be formed. A wide receiver should use the scoop formed by his arms and hands to catch and absorb a pass that's thrown below his waist.

If a pass is thrown below his knees, a wide receiver should be prepared to lower his arms and hands to ground level to trap the football between his arms and hands and stomach. To perform a knee-level or lower catch, a wide receiver should use the pinkies in, thumbs out technique. As a wide receiver lowers his body to the ground to catch a pass thrown below knee level, his arms and hands should be positioned between the football and the ground. Proper positioning of his hands and arms will form the bottom part of a basket, which is used for the football to land in. The basket's upper part is formed by a wide receiver's chest and stomach. If the scoop technique is properly performed, then the football should be securely trapped between a wide receiver's arms and hands and his stomach and chest, which will keep the football from touching the ground.

Figure 2-2. The pinkies are facing inward and the thumbs are extended out when attempting to catch a pass thrown below waist level.

Over-the-Shoulder Catching Techniques

Catching a pass thrown over a wide receiver's shoulder can be a difficult task to accomplish. To perform this task, a wide receiver should have great concentration and be able to track the football with his eyes and head while still running at full speed. When catching a pass thrown over his shoulder like a fade route or streak route, a wide receiver should use the pinkies in, thumbs out technique (Figure 2-3). What makes the over-the-shoulder catch difficult is the process of twisting the head and eyes with the football's flight. When the football leaves the quarterback's hand, a wide receiver should be able to turn his head back to the football and track the football's flight path. As the football reaches the hands, a wide receiver should be able to turn his head and eyes with the football's flight and watch the football land in his hands and be successfully secured in a tuck position. During the football's flight, a wide receiver should never take his eyes off the football's path.

When performing an over-the-shoulder catch, a wide receiver should always attempt to catch the football at its highest point. This term is called *high pointing* the football. Catching the football at its highest point makes it difficult for a defensive back to shoot his hands through the football and break up a pass. Catching the football at

Figure 2-3. When catching a pass thrown over a wide receivers shoulder, his hands should be flipped with the pinkies in and the thumbs out. Also when catching a pass thrown over his shoulder a wide receiver should always catch the ball at the highest possible point.

its lowest point makes it easier for a defensive back to shoot his hands and break up a pass. When attempting to perform an over-the-shoulder catch, a wide receiver should also remember to extend his arms and hands to the football at the last possible second before the football lands. Extending the arms and hands late will allow a wide receiver to maintain full speed all the way through the catch. Extending the arms early will cause a wide receiver to slow down and not be able to accelerate through the catch.

Pocket Catching Techniques

The pocket catch technique is the safest and surest method a wide receiver can use to catch a pass. Using the pocket catch allows a wide receiver to secure the football as soon as the ball touches his body. The pocket catch is a great alternative to using the pinkies in technique, which can be awkward to perform in certain situations. The pocket catch is also a great technique to use when the ball is wet.

Using the pocket catch technique, a wide receiver traps the football in between his upper arm and rib cage because the football is wedged into the armpit. The combination and position of a wide receiver's upper arm, rib cage, and armpit create a natural pocket for the football to land into (Figure 2-4). The upper arm and rib cage create the pocket's

Figure 2-4. The upper arm, rib cage, and armpit create a natural pocket for the football to land into. The hands act as a funnel to the pocket when performing a pocket catch.

sides and the armpit acts as the backstop for the football to land into. When a wide receiver performs the pocket catch, his hands should be hyperextended and shouldn't obstruct the football's flight into the pocket being formed by his upper arm and rib cage. During the pocket catch, a wide receiver's hands are used to funnel the football to the pocket. The hands should secure the football upon impact of the ball landing in the pocket.

To correctly perform a pocket catch, a wide receiver should correctly align his body with the football's flight. The pocket formed by the upper arm and rib cage should be aligned with the football's flight. To ensure the pocket's correct alignment, a wide receiver may have to adjust his running speed to the football's flight. Correctly aligning the pocket with the football's flight may cause a wide receiver to speed up, slow down, jump, or dive to correctly perform a pocket catch.

One-Handed Catching Techniques

Sometimes, when trying to perform a catch, a pass might be thrown so far away that a wide receiver can only manage to attempt to catch the pass with one hand. Catching the football with one hand is much like catching the football with two hands: A wide receiver should use his one free hand to perform a basket-like catch. The fingers should be spread as far as possible without making the hand too stiff. The middle finger acts as the basket's back and the rest of the fingers and thumb form the basket's sides. When positioned correctly, the fingers should help cushion the football from hitting the palm of the hand. The fingers should help a wide receiver rip the football out of the air when performing a one-handed catch.

When performing a one-handed catch, a wide receiver should use his arm to cushion and secure the football upon impact. The off hand should be used to secure the football as soon as it's in a position to support the hand that's performing the catch. When hitting the ground, a wide receiver should try not to fall on his elbow, which will cause the football to jar loose. Instead, a wide receiver should try to roll upon contact with the ground to absorb the blow and prevent the football from jarring loose.

Behind-the-Body Catching Techniques

When a pass is thrown behind a wide receiver's body, a wide receiver should be ready to use the pocket catch technique to make a reception. The pocket catch is a great technique to use for a pass thrown behind a wide receiver. Like in a normal pocket catch, the upper arm, rib cage, and armpit create a natural pocket for the ball to land into. The lower arm or opposite arm from where the pocket is being formed should now shoot across the body and act as the pocket's lower part when a pass is thrown behind a wide receiver. The hands still act as a funnel to the pocket and secure the football upon its arrival in the pocket.

The key element to catching a pass thrown behind a wide receiver is great body control. Having great body control will allow a wide receiver to twist and contort his whole body toward the pass's direction. A wide receiver should be able to control and twist his torso toward the direction the football is coming from when a pass is thrown behind him. A wide receiver's hip to the football's flight side should be opened toward the direction to which the football is being thrown (Figure 2-5). Opening the hip toward the football's flight will allow a wide receiver's entire body to twist toward the football's direction. Opening the hip toward the football's flight will make it easier for a wide receiver to extend his arms toward the football and perform a pocket catch. Also, when preparing to make a reception on a pass thrown behind a wide receiver, a wide receiver should be ready to slow down or even stop to make it easier for his body to twist and contort toward the direction of the football's flight.

Figure 2-5. The hip to the football's flight side should open, allowing the torso and arms to twist back toward the football to perform a pocket catch technique on a pass thrown behind a wide receiver.

Sideline Catching Techniques

In junior high school, high school, and college football, a wide receiver has to have only one foot inbounds for a pass to be considered complete. It's imperative that coaches make sure their wide receivers understand this notion and that they practice proper sideline catching techniques and drills. Trying to get both feet inbounds can cause a wide receiver to turn a catchable pass into an incompletion by not executing proper sideline catching techniques.

Similar to performing a catch thrown behind him, when a wide receiver attempts to catch a pass thrown near the sideline or out-of-bounds, he should demonstrate great body control. When attempting a sideline catch, a wide receiver should use whatever catching technique is necessary to make the catch. If the pass is thrown over his shoulder, then a wide receiver should use an over-the-shoulder catch and ensure to catch the football at its highest point. If the ball is thrown at shoulder level, a wide receiver should use a shoulder-level or pocket catch technique. Executing the proper footwork on the sideline is what will make the difference in a reception or an incompletion for a wide receiver attempting a sideline catch.

When a wide receiver is trying to make a sideline catch, the hydra technique should be used to properly execute the catch (Figure 2-6). The near leg to the football's flight should be kicked out into the air toward the sideline. The foot of the near leg should be flexed down toward the ground, ensuring a wide receiver lands on the ball of his foot. The kick-out or hydra action of the near foot will cause the back foot to drag behind the near leg. The back foot should be flexed down toward the ground; the flexed action will help the back foot achieve the desired dragging action. Properly executing the hydra technique will cause the back foot to drag, ensuring the wide receiver has one foot inbounds, which will result in a reception.

Figure 2-6. The near foot should kick out toward the sideline, causing the back foot to drag to execute the hydra technique.

Catching Drills

Drill #1: Down the Line: Over-the-Shoulder and Wrong-Shoulder Catches

The down-the-line drill (Figure 2-7) is a great way to warm up wide receivers pre-practice or in individual practice time. The down-the-line drill incorporates many different types of catches a wide receiver has to make throughout a game. The first wide receiver starts the drill when he sees the coach snap the football. The coach throws an over-the-shoulder pass to a wide receiver, who's running three-quarter speed down the field. The wide receiver should make an over-the-shoulder catch to finish the repetition. The over-the-shoulder pass is repeated so a catch is made from each side of a wide receiver's body. Next, the coach moves directly behind the group of wide receivers and throws an over-the-shoulder pass to a wide receiver's wrong shoulder. The wrong-shoulder pass makes a wide receiver have to track the football with his eyes without breaking eye contact with the football. The wrong-shoulder throw should be repeated on the way back so each wide receiver gets a catch from both sides. The final throw in the over-the-shoulder series is for the coach to make an over-the-shoulder throw and for a wide receiver to make a one-handed over the shoulder catch with his outside hand. Once everyone has caught a pass with each outside hand, then the coach should make an over-the-shoulder pass and each wide receiver will make a one-handed catch with his inside hand.

Coaching Points

When attempting to make a catch on an over-the-shoulder pass, a wide receiver needs to catch the football at its highest point. Catching the football at its lowest point will make it easier for a defender to shoot his hands and break up the pass. On the wrong-shoulder throw, a wide receiver needs to track the football with his eyes and adjust to the football's flight. His head and eyes need to twist and adjust with the football's flight to make a catch. For the one-handed catch to the outside hand, a wide receiver needs to create a basket with his back hand. The middle finger acts as the basket's backstop, which will allow the rest of the fingers to tighten around the football to secure the pass. For the one-handed catch with the inside hand, a wide receiver needs to attempt to rip the football out of the air with his inside hand. The fingers of the inside hand need to be spread wide and will tighten around the football.

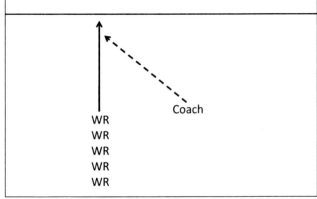

Figure 2-7. Down-the-line drill: over-the-shoulder and wrong-shoulder catches

Drill #2: Down the Line: Over-the-Head, Below-the-Waist, and Out-to-the-Side Catches

In the second part of the down-the-line drill (Figure 2-8), the wide receivers face the coach and then run right at the coach at the snap of the ball. The coach throws an over-the-head pass to the first wide receiver. Once the wide receiver catches the football, he should plant off his near foot and knife upfield. The over-the-head pass is repeated, then the coach moves on to a below-the-waist throw. Once a catch is made by a wide receiver, he should knife upfield and get back in line to wait for the drill to be repeated. After the below-the-waist throw, the coach should then throw the ball to each wide receiver's side. Again, after making the catch, the wide receiver should knife upfield.

Coaching Points

For the over-the-head catch, a wide receiver should remember to track the football with his eyes and squeeze the ball with his fingertips, which will tighten the noose around the football. An over-the-head catch should always be caught at the football's highest point with the thumbs in and pinkies out. For the below-the-waist catch, a wide receiver should be reminded that he's probably going to have to sink his hips to get his hands to the level of the football's flight path. The football should be caught with the pinkies in and thumbs out. The arms and elbows should be in tight, forming a basket for the football to land into. When making a catch on the pass thrown to his side, a wide receiver should be reminded that the football can either be caught with a noose catch or a pocket catch. If using a pocket catch, a wide receiver needs to be reminded to align his pocket with the football's flight path. Coaches also need to keep reminding wide receivers to stick a foot in the ground and knife upfield to complete the drill properly.

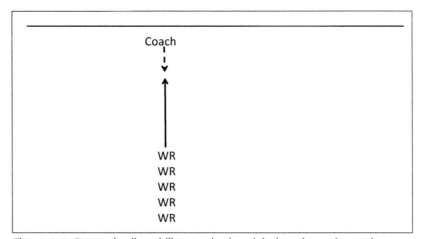

Figure 2-8. Down-the-line drill: over-the-head, below-the-waist, and out-to-the-side catches

Drill #3: Noose Catching

The noose catching drill (Figure 2-9) is another great way to warm up wide receivers' hands and eyes. Each wide receiver should get a partner and align eight yards apart. One partner throws the football to the wide receiver. Each wide receiver catches three passes directly at him and above his head. After these two, a wide receiver will turn to his right and catch three passes in a row, then he'll turn to his left and do the same thing. After completing this rotation, the partners switch places and repeat. This drill is designed for wide receivers to practice perfect technique when making a noose catch.

Coaching Points

When attempting a noose catch, a wide receiver should spread his fingers wide and catch the football with his fingertips. As the football hits a wide receiver's hands, the fingers should tighten the noose around the football so no defender can knock the ball from a wide receiver's hands. When practicing the noose catch drill, wide receivers need to be reminded to step toward and attack the football with their feet. This will help wide receivers develop a sense of urgency and aggression when attempting to catch the football.

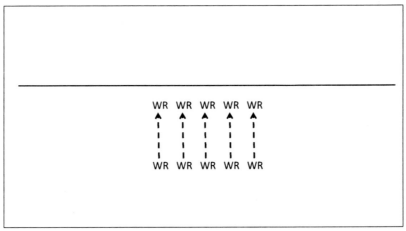

Figure 2-9. Noose catching drill

Drill #4: Distraction

The distraction drill (Figure 2-10) is designed to help a wide receiver concentrate on the football's flight when defenders are crossing his path. The wide receivers need to be divided into two lines for this drill. One line is designated as the wide receiver and the other line is the distracter. At the snap of the football, a wide receiver will run behind the distracter, who's moving in the opposite direction. The coach will stand 10 yards away from the wide receiver and throw through the distracter to him. The distracter will try to make it difficult for the wide receiver to catch the pass without hitting the ball.

Coaching Points

To accomplish this drill, a wide receiver needs to develop great concentration and eye placement. Coaches should remind wide receivers to find a spot on the football to focus their eyes on. A wide receiver can focus his eyes either on the white stripe or the football's front tip. Also, when catching a pass in traffic, a wide receiver should look the football all the way into the tuck position to secure the catch properly.

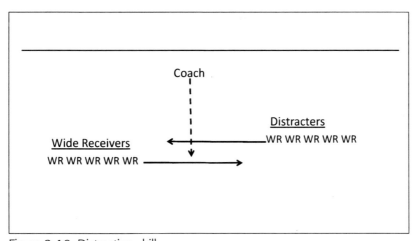

Figure 2-10. Distraction drill

Drill #5: Blur

The blur drill (Figure 2-11) is designed to help a wide receiver improve his concentration when catching the football. Two players align a yard apart from each other and wave their hands in front of the football without touching the ball, offering a distraction for a wide receiver. At the snap of the football, a wide receiver runs behind the two distracters and attempts to catch the football. To add variation to the drill, coaches can have their wide receivers run different pass routes, such as a curl route, and put the distraction at the point in the pass route where a wide receiver would catch the football.

Coaching Points

To accomplish this drill, a wide receiver needs to develop great concentration and eye placement. Coaches should remind wide receivers to find a spot on the football to focus their eyes on. A wide receiver can focus his eyes either on the white stripe or the football's front tip. Also, when catching a pass in traffic, a wide receiver should look the football all the way into the tuck position to secure the catch properly.

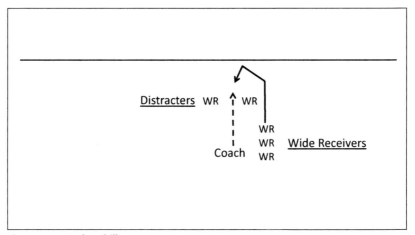

Figure 2-11. Blur drill

Drill #6: Sandwich

The sandwich drill (Figure 2-12) is designed to teach a wide receiver to go up and high-point the football when he's in traffic. The wide receiver stands between two other players, who are one foot away from him. At the snap of the football, the wide receiver makes one fake and runs either right or left and tries to catch a jump ball throw from the coach. The other two players try to keep the wide receiver from making the catch by blocking his vision and lightly pushing him.

Coaching Points

The sandwich drill will teach wide receivers to go up in traffic and catch a jump ball throw at its highest point. When attempting to catch a jump ball throw, a wide receiver needs to focus his eyes on either the white stripe or the football's front tip. A wide receiver shouldn't let the distracter's actions during the sandwich drill break his concentration. Also, to make this type of catch, a wide receiver should always catch the football at its highest point and away from the distracter's hands.

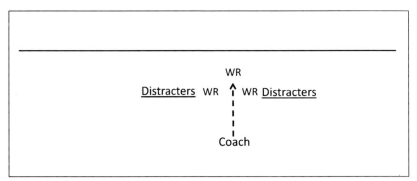

Figure 2-12. Sandwich drill

Drill #7: Bag Harass

The bag harass drill (Figure 2-13) is designed to help a wide receiver maintain total concentration on catching the football when he knows he's going to be hit by a defender as soon as he catches the football. To begin the drill, a player needs to grab a bag, and as soon as a wide receiver catches the football, the bag holder hits him with the bag. To add variation to the drill, the coach can have the wide receivers run different routes and have the bag holder stand where the wide receiver would catch the pass.

Coaching Points

To accomplish this drill, a wide receiver needs to develop great concentration and eye placement. Coaches should remind wide receivers to find a spot on the football to focus their eyes on. A wide receiver can focus his eyes either on the white stripe or the football's front tip. Also, when catching a pass in traffic, a wide receiver should look the football all the way into the tuck position to secure the catch properly. To successfully make a catch in traffic, a wide receiver should never look at the defender; instead, he needs to concentrate on the football but prepare his body for contact by using his body to shield the defender from the football.

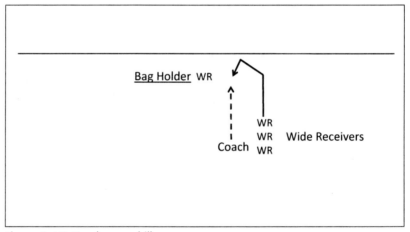

Figure 2-13. Bag harass drill

Drill #8: Hydra Sideline Catch

The hydra sideline catch drill (Figure 2-14) is designed for a wide receiver to practice his hydra sideline catch technique. A line of wide receivers will run at the sideline one at a time and the coach will throw a pass at the sideline to force a wide receiver to use his hydra technique to make the catch. To add variation, a coach can use the back corner of the end zone to practice over-the-shoulder hydra catches.

Coaching Points

It's imperative that a wide receiver be forced to hydra during this drill. When attempting a hydra sideline catch, a wide receiver should kick his inside leg out toward the sideline, which will cause his back foot to drag across the field. The dragging action of the back foot will ensure that a wide receiver gets one foot inbounds to ensure the completion of the pass.

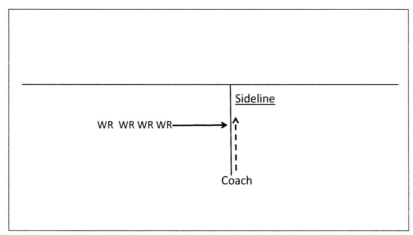

Figure 2-14. Hydra sideline catch drill

3

Wide Receiver Stance and Start Fundamentals

To create a great building, the foundation should be solidly established. The building of a great wide receiver should begin by talking about the very first thing a wide receiver does before the start of every play. This chapter will start with a discussion about the stance and start, which is the foundation of any great wide receiver.

A great stance is an aspect to playing the wide receiver position that many coaches neglect. If a player doesn't know how to assume the proper stance, the timing of his play can be greatly disrupted. Great offensive football is all about precision and timing. If the slot wide receiver false-steps out of his stance, it might cost him a half second and mean the difference between a completion and an incompletion. In the run game, stepping with the wrong foot out of his stance can be the difference in whether the split end can get into a position to block a quarter's coverage safety. Little mistakes like these over the course of a game can be the difference between a wide receiver being an effective and efficient player or being ineffective and inefficient executing his assignments.

The wide receiver position is a versatile athletic position that accommodates many different speeds, skill sets, and body types. At the beginning of a coach's first practice, the wide receiver stance is the first thing every coach should focus on no matter what level. College coaches should keep in mind they might have recruited a high school player who's never played the wide receiver position before. This can be a very common practice. High school quarterbacks are often the quarterbacks of their teams because they're great athletes. Such high school quarterbacks often make great wide receivers. When coaching at the high school level, coaches have an even greater chance of dealing with a player who's never played the wide receiver position before. Never assume a player knows how to get into a proper stance or execute a proper start. He might think he does. However, a player's stance more than likely won't be sound and efficient. Coaches should show their wide receivers exactly how they want their wide receivers to get into their stances. In addition, it never hurts for veteran players to hear a coach teach stance fundamentals once again. He might be able to remind his wide receivers about something they've been neglecting. This gives the position coach a chance to revaluate the important skills and fundamentals of playing the wide receiver position.

Wide Receiver Stance Techniques

The wide receiver stance is a staggered two-point stance very similar to a track sprinter's stance. Each player should be able to explode out of his stance as fast as possible to get into a pass route or to be able to get off the line of scrimmage quickly to put himself in a position to execute a run block.

Stance Foot Fundamentals

When coaches teach the stance, they should start by having the athlete assume an athletic position. His knees should be bent slightly and his feet should be hip-width apart. Next, the athlete puts this lead foot forward about 12 inches in front of his back foot. Taller players can take more of a stagger in their stance due to their longer legs. Shorter players might have less of a stagger. For balance, the lead foot is turned slightly inward. About 80 percent of the athlete's weight should be placed on the ball of the lead foot, and 20 percent of his weight should be on the back foot (Figure 3-1). If enough weight is on the front foot, a wide receiver will naturally move forward powerfully at the snap of the ball, exploding the back foot forward without false-stepping. If a wide receiver has a problem with false-stepping, adding more weight to the front foot can alleviate the problem. At the snap of the ball, the extra weight on the front foot will give the back foot only one choice—and that's to move forward without false-stepping.

A number of theories exist about deciding which foot to put forward in a wide receiver's stance. The most common is to have the inside foot forward (Figure 3-1). Teams that use steps for pass timing usually prefer the inside foot up. Another way to decide which foot to put forward is to use an assignment-based thought. In this theory, the lead foot is predicated on the assignment. For example, if a slot wide receiver needs to execute a cutoff block on an alley defender playing to the inside of him, he should make the outside foot the lead foot so his first step is with his inside foot and is directly at the alley defender (Figure 3-2). This technique can help the slot execute his block a step quicker than if his inside foot is the lead foot. If the slot is running a three-step slant route, he'd want the inside foot forward so that on his third step, he could plant his outside foot and properly execute a slant route.

Figure 3-1. This figure shows the starting point of the wide receiver stance. The lead foot is about 12 inches in front of the back foot. The lead foot is pointed slightly inward, with 80 percent of the weight on the lead foot and 20 percent of the weight on the back foot.

Figure 3-2. This figure shows the outside foot as the lead foot and the inside foot as the back foot. The outside foot lead foot stance can reduce the time it takes a wide receiver to block a defender who's aligned inside of him.

The final theory about deciding which foot to have as lead foot is to have the outside foot the lead foot at all times (Figure 3-1). This provides the benefit of being able to attack and cut off an inside defender a step quicker. In addition, having the outside foot as the lead foot all the time doesn't give away assignments to defenders based on which foot is the lead foot. This method does have a possible major drawback: Having the outside foot as the lead foot will add an extra step to inward-breaking timed pass routes. For example, with the outside foot as the lead foot, a three-step slant route will now take four steps to execute. The fourth step will be when the outside foot is ready to break inward to execute the slant route. When deciding which foot to make the lead foot, coaches should make a decision based on which theory best fits the parameters of their offense.

Arm Stance Fundamentals

In the wide receiver stance, the arms should be relaxed and placed at stomach level. The elbows should be bent at a 90-degree angle and ready to explode forward at the snap of the ball. This will help enable great running form for a wide receiver. The hands and fingers should be loose and relaxed. If the hands are tense, the whole body will be tense. This will cause a wide receiver to be slower out of his stance. Wide receivers should think of their arms as weapons and should always strive to keep their arms in a fighting position, which is above stomach level. If a wide receiver drops his arms below the stomach level, he leaves his body open for a defender to strike him. To sustain proper arm placement throughout a play, a wide receiver should start with them above stomach level. When facing press coverage, a wide receiver should make sure his hands and arms are above the pressed defender's hands and arms (Figure 3-3). Having the hands above the defender's hands assures a wide receiver that he'll have better leverage over the defensive back. Better leverage and proper hand placement above stomach level allow a wide receiver to strike the defender's hands at a downward angle, which makes it easier to achieve a good release from press coverage.

Figure 3-3. This figure shows the proper hand leverage of a wide receiver when facing press coverage. The wide receiver's hands are above the defenders hands. The wide receiver's hands can strike the defender's hands at a downward angle.

Body Stance Fundamentals

A wide receiver should align with a slight body lean in his stance. If aligned correctly, the shoulders are over the front knee and the front knee is aligned over the toes of the lead foot. A wide receiver should be able to draw an imaginary line from his nose down to his front foot. If he can do this, then perfect body lean has been achieved (Figure 3-4). In his stance, a wide receiver should be relaxed and have a well-gathered carriage. He doesn't want a loose, unfocused carriage in his stance. However, a wide receiver doesn't want a tight carriage that doesn't allow him to smoothly release off the line of scrimmage.

Figure 3-4. This figure shows the proper body lean of a wide receiver in his stance. The shoulders are aligned over the front knee and the front knee is aligned over the toes of the lead foot.

Head and Eye Stance Fundamentals

Before the snap of the football, a wide receiver needs to use his eyes to scan the field to identify the safeties on the field. Once the safeties are identified, a wide receiver needs to indentify the defender over the top of him. The process a wide receiver performs before the snap of every play is called the *pre-snap scan*. A wide receiver uses the pre-snap scan to analyze the defense's alignment to identify the defensive scheme being run by the opponent. After the pre-snap scan, the eyes and head should be up and turned in at a 45-degree angle, watching for the snap of the ball. In addition, a wide receiver should be trying to eyeball any late defensive movement. When dealing with younger wide receivers, a coach should first have them watch the football prior to the snap. This will ensure a wide receiver only releases when he sees ball movement. A young wide receiver should understand early the learning process that he releases off the line of scrimmage on the snap of the ball, not on the quarterback's cadence sound. After learning to get off the line of scrimmage on ball movement, a young wide receiver can learn to watch the football and defensive movement. Remember, the farther a wide receiver aligns from the ball, the harder it is for him to hear the snap count. This makes it imperative for a wide receiver to watch the football to get off on time.

Stance Variety

When coaches teach the stance, they should keep in mind that each individual's stance is going to be slightly different. Players should be comfortable and relaxed in their stances because they might have to stay in it for long periods of time before the football is finally snapped. However, a wide receiver shouldn't be so relaxed that he assumes a high stance. Achieving a comfortably low stance is good terminology to use when coaches try to get this thought across to their players. Also, it's imperative a wide receiver assumes the same stance whether it's run or pass. A wide receiver doesn't want to give away the play by changing his stance for run or pass.

Wide Receiver Alignment Concepts

Before a wide receiver can even take his stance, he should first know where on the field he should be and how to line up. An offense's split rules can vary greatly by formation and play call design. A general rule that all wide receivers can remember is to crowd the line of scrimmage as best they can. A wide receiver on the ball should align as close to the line of scrimmage as possible without being offside. A wide receiver properly aligned in the backfield should crowd the line of scrimmage as much as possible. A wide receiver aligned in the backfield should remember to check with an official to make sure he's properly aligned in the backfield. Crowding the line of scrimmage allows a wide receiver to threaten the defense vertically as quickly as possible at the snap of the ball. This greatly helps the passing game's overall effectiveness. When facing press coverage, a wide receiver off the ball can take an extra step back off the line of scrimmage to create extra room to execute a release versus press coverage. This is one of the few instances when a wide receiver wouldn't want to crowd the line of scrimmage.

Wide Receiver Starts

After a wide receiver learns how to get into a proper stance and where to align on the field, the next step for him is to learn how to explode out of his stance without any wasted movement. A wide receiver leaving his stance should have the same mindset of a sprinter who's about to run the 100-meter dash. The sprinter wants to explode out of his stance low and accelerate as quickly as possible to full speed with a gradual raise of the body until a full-speed carriage is reached. To accomplish such sprint run action, a wide receiver needs proper get-off, arm action, and head and eye usage.

Wide Receiver Get-Off

At the snap of the ball, a wide receiver should press off the front foot and pop the back foot through as quickly as possible without any false steps or negative movement. With a proper get-off, a wide receiver can correctly pop the back foot through low and quick to generate maximum push off the lead foot. This action will lead to a low, powerful get-off. The first step out of the stance should be low and cover eight to 12 inches. For a taller wide receiver, the first step might be slightly longer than it would be for a shorter wide receiver. The first step is designed to be a powerful quick movement that propels the athlete out of his stance and into his play assignment. A wide receiver doesn't want to overstride on the first step. Overstriding, or overextending, out of his stance can cause a wide receiver to take a longer amount of time to accelerate to full speed. After the first step, a wide receiver should work to gain as much ground as possible while striving to reach full speed. The second step should be longer than the first step. The steps should increase gradually to full speed or to the breakpoint of the assigned route. During the get-off, a wide receiver's body should be driving forward at an approximate 45-degree angle lean. The lean will help propel the legs quicker and keep a wide receiver's body from rising up. The goal of a great get-off should be for a wide receiver to reach full speed by his third step or to at least give off the illusion that he's reached full speed to the defense by the third step.

An efficient wide receiver should have the same get-off every play—no matter if it's a run or a pass. With this thought in mind, a wide receiver should also understand how to take the appropriate angle of departure to execute his assignment. If a wide receiver is a split end and it's his job to block a quarter's coverage safety, he can't release straight up the field and still expect to effectively execute his assignment. Instead, a wide receiver should release flat at an angle that allows him to get into a proper position to accomplish his assignment.

Wide Receiver Arm Usage

Just as in executing proper foot action, a wide receiver's arms should explode forward out of the stance. A wide receiver initially moves the opposite arm of the initial step foot and attempts to execute a well-gathered but smooth running form during the get-off. The arms should be bent at the elbow, creating a 90-degree angle. The arms should swing tight to the body. A wide receiver doesn't want the elbows to get wide during the get-off or throughout the pass route. Wide elbows will cause a wide receiver's arm swing to cut across his body. An across-the-body arm swing will slow down a wide receiver's get-off. During the get-off and throughout the play, a wide receiver doesn't want to drop his hands below stomach level. A wide receiver's hands should be up at all times to ward off a defender's jamming action and to catch the ball.

When executing shorter routes, such as a three-step slant or a five-step hitch, a wide receiver should overexaggerate his arm movements during the get-off. This will help give the illusion that he's running a streak route to the defensive back or at least some form of deeper route.

Wide Receiver Head and Eyes Start Fundamentals

A wide receiver's head and eyes should remain up at all times during a wide receiver's start and get-off. A wide receiver should be able to identify and analyze the defense and its movement before and after the snap. This task can't be accomplished if a wide receiver's head and eyes are down. During the get-off, a wide receiver should use his eyes to scan the defensive secondary. During the initial phase of a play, wide receivers should be able to see the cornerback over the top of them and the safety to their near hash. Slot receivers should be able to see the safety lined up over them and the alley defender aligned to their inside or outside. If a wide receiver's head and eyes are down during the first three steps of a wide receiver's get-off, the defensive coverage can be extremely hard to identify.

Drills for the Stance and Start

At the start of an individual period, coaches can use one of these drills to work the stance and start. The drills presented are all great ways to warm up the body while also working to perfect a wide receiver's techniques. As the season wears on, the stance and start tend to be forgotten and neglected. It's imperative to take the time to incorporate one of these drills into an individual practice period. Players should understand how important it is to have a great stance and start if they want to become effective wide receivers.

Drill #1: Get-Offs

This drill is designed to work on a wide receiver's start (Figure 3-5). Have all wide receivers get in one long line and stand one arm's width apart. The coach will pick a side and have the wide receivers get off on ball movement and burst through 10 yards. On the way back, the wide receivers should switch their lead foot (from the inside foot to the outside foot).

Coaching Points

- The wide receiver shouldn't take any false steps.
- His eyes should be inside, watching for ball movement.
- The wide receiver should take a quick first step (not overstride).
- He should fire low and hard out of his stance.
- His eyes should be up, focused on the secondary.
- The wide receiver should finish through 10 yards.

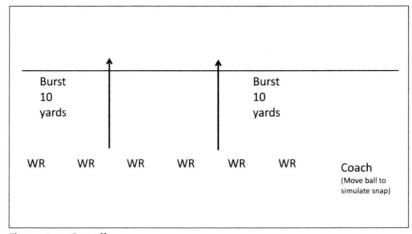

Figure 3-5. Get-offs

Drill #2: Angled Get-Offs

This drill is designed to work on a wide receiver's stance and start (Figure 3-6). The wide receivers will make their outside foot the lead foot and get off on ball movement. At the snap of the ball, a wide receiver will release at a 45-degree angle, stepping with the inside foot first. This drill is designed to simulate a wide receiver releasing to execute a cutoff or convoy block or a drag route. The wide receivers finish through 10 yards.

Coaching Points

- The wide receiver shouldn't take any false steps.
- His eyes should be inside, watching for ball movement.
- The wide receiver should take a flat first step (not gaining a lot of ground).
- He should fire low and hard out of his stance.
- His eyes should be up, focused on the secondary.
- The wide receiver should finish through 10 yards.

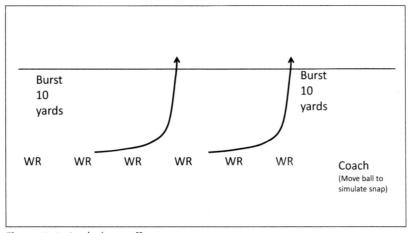

Figure 3-6. Angled get-offs

Drill #3: Eyes Up Get-Offs

This drill is designed to work on a wide receiver's stance and start (Figure 3-7). A wide receiver fires out of his stance on ball movement with his eyes up and on the coach. The coach holds up any combination of fingers. The wide receiver shouts out the number of fingers the coach holds up and finishes through 10 yards. If only one coach is available, then have the wide receivers get off on a snap count. Also, the coach should move around during this drill to simulate defensive movement. This will train a wide receiver's eyes during the start to find the defensive back.

Coaching Points

- The wide receiver shouldn't take any false steps.
- His eyes should be inside, watching for ball movement.
- The wide receiver should keep his eyes up during start (recognizing defensive movement).
- He should fire low and hard out of his stance.
- His eyes should be up, focused on the secondary.
- The wide receiver should finish through 10 yards.

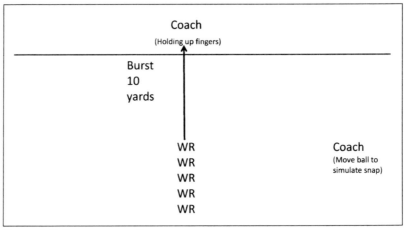

Figure 3-7. Eyes up get-offs

Drill #4: Burst Through Me

This drill is designed to work on a wide receiver's stance and start (Figure 3-8). A wide receiver fires out of his stance on ball movement with his eyes up and on the coach. As the wide receiver fires out, the coach tosses a ball low. The wide receiver should burst through the ball with great running form. If the wide receiver doesn't get off the ball with great effort, he'll never be able to burst through the ball. This drill can be done from five yards away or from 10 years away. The coach can vary his distance to offer changes in the drill.

Coaching Points

- The wide receiver shouldn't take any false steps.
- His eyes should be inside, watching for ball movement.
- The wide receiver should keep his eyes up during start (recognizing defensive movement).
- He should fire low and hard out of his stance.
- His eyes should be up, focused on the secondary.
- The wide receiver should finish through the ball.

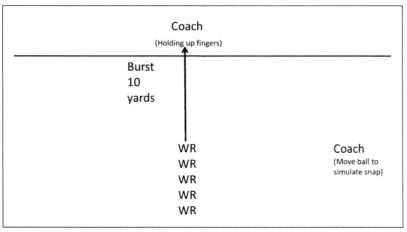

Figure 3-8. Burst through me

4

Wide Receiver Releases

After a wide receiver develops a great stance and start, the next fundamental he should master is learning how to escape off the line of scrimmage by using a release. In the game of football today, more teams are playing press coverage defensive schemes than ever before. Teams are using a variety of different zone press coverages and man press coverages to make it difficult for wide receivers to release off the line of scrimmage and to disrupt the timing of an offense's passing game. With all the different types of press coverage defenses are playing, a wide receiver should be able to win at the line of scrimmage with a great release.

The release phase for a wide receiver is between the line of scrimmage and five yards down the field. The release phase is when a wide receiver should concentrate on achieving a clean release against a defender who's pressing him. If a wide receiver hasn't beaten a pressed defender after five yards, he's likely not going to win his pass route against a defender. Obtaining a clean release during the release phase of his pass route requires a wide receiver to work through the five keys of a clean release:

- Analyzing and mentally preparing
- Having a low center of gravity
- Using speed and quickness
- Being aggressive
- Being deceptive

When a wide receiver understands how to use the five keys to obtain a successful release from the line of scrimmage, he'll be armed with the tools necessary to win his pass route against a defender every time he sees a version of press coverage.

Five Keys of a Clean Release

Analyzing and Mentally Preparing Release Fundamentals

The first key to being successful against press coverage is for a wide receiver to analyze a defender's posture pre-snap and to use that information to mentally prepare himself to face press coverage. Before the start of every play, a wide receiver should scan the field to identify the defense's pre-snap alignment. As mentioned in Chapter 3, this is called the *pre-snap scan*. Using his pre-snap scan, a wide receiver will be able to identify if he's going to face press coverage. If a wide receiver is going to see press coverage, a defender will be aligned directly over the top of him anywhere from one yard to five yards off the line of scrimmage. The closer a defender aligns will tell a wide receiver that the defender plans to play hard press coverage. If the defender is aligned farther away than one yard off the line of scrimmage, he's probably going to play soft press coverage. A wide receiver should be able to recognize the difference between a defender using hard press coverage or soft press coverage if he's going to execute a successful release.

To understand how a defender plays, a wide receiver should spend time watching film of his opponent throughout the week leading up to the football game. A wide receiver should be able to identify a defender's tendencies and weaknesses to prepare himself to face press coverage. Watching film will help a wide receiver prepare for the type of coverage scheme his opponent uses when it plays press coverage. From watching film, a wide receiver will also be able to understand how each opposing defender likes to play press coverage. Mentally preparing himself for press coverage throughout the week leading up to the game will give a wide receiver an advantage over a defender who hasn't watched much film throughout the week. On game day, when a wide receiver sees press coverage, he'll be ready to exploit a defender's weaknesses and win his individual pass route.

Using the information gathered from watching opponent film and from his pre-snap scan, a wide receiver will be able to analyze and identify if he's going to see press coverage on an upcoming play. Once a wide receiver identifies press coverage from the defense, the next step to execute a successful release is to formulate a plan of attack. Once a wide receiver knows that press coverage is imminent, his plan of attack should be developed quickly. From watching film all week, a wide receiver should make a list of four to five different releases he feels will work against a defender when he sees press coverage. A wide receiver's list should include a release to beat every variation of press coverage an opponent is going to run against him that week. Preparing a release list each week for an opponent will ensure he'll be ready to face press coverage on game day. Using his release list, a wide receiver should quickly know what his plan of attack is for press coverage throughout an entire game. If an opponent uses press coverage unexpectedly, then the wide receiver's plan of attack should revert to his best release if the release is appropriate given a defender's leverage and position. Keeping a release list will prepare a wide receiver to always have a plan of attack when he faces press coverage.

For a wide receiver to be prepared to beat press coverage on game day, he should combine his film study throughout the week leading up to his game with the information gathered during his pre-snap scan. Using this combination of information, a wide receiver should formulate a plan of attack to beat press coverage. If a wide receiver can correctly analyze a defender's technique and use his prepared release list to his advantage, then he'll be able to obtain a clean, successful release from the line of scrimmage.

Low Center of Gravity Release Fundamentals

Once a wide receiver has analyzed a defender and formulated a plan of attack for his release, he can concentrate on the second key to obtaining a successful release: keeping a low center of gravity throughout his release phase. To accomplish this, a wide receiver should narrow his stance and not expose his chest to a pressed defender.

As a wide receiver identifies press coverage during his pre-snap scan, the first thing he should do after formulating a plan is to narrow his stance (Figure 4-1). For a wide

Figure 4-1. Against a pressed defender, a wide receiver should narrow his stance. A wide receiver doesn't want as much stagger in his stance so he can get his feet under his body quicker.

receiver to narrow his stance, he should reduce the stagger in his stance. Reducing the stagger will allow a wide receiver's feet to be positioned under his body quicker than normal upon the snap of the football. Having his feet positioned under his body will help a wide receiver execute his release more efficiently when facing press coverage.

Once a wide receiver has narrowed his stance, he can concentrate on keeping his center of gravity low and not exposing his chest to a defender during the release phase. In his narrowed stance, a wide receiver should bend his knees and keep a positive forward body lean. Against press, if a wide receiver is leaning back in his stance, his center of gravity will be too high, exposing his chest to the pressed defender. Pressed defenders are taught to aim for a wide receiver's chest when attempting to jam him. A wide receiver can counteract a defender's coaching by playing with a low pad level, thereby keeping his center of gravity low. Having a low center of gravity will more than likely cause a defender to hit a wide receiver's shoulder pads instead of his chest when attempting to jam a wide receiver. Not exposing his chest to a defender—accompanied with narrowing his stance—will help a wide receiver keep a low center of gravity throughout his release phase.

Speed and Quickness Release Fundamentals

Once a wide receiver has a plan of attack to beat press coverage and is keeping his pad level low, he can then concentrate on the third key to obtaining a release against press coverage: using speed and quickness to his advantage during the release phase of his pass route. Having great speed or quickness is a critical attribute to have against press coverage. For a wide receiver to fully utilize his speed and quickness, he should understand how to use these attributes to his advantage when he's facing press coverage. To use his speed and quickness correctly against press coverage, a wide receiver should keep an internal clock, use quick concise hand and foot movements, and always threaten a defender vertically down the field.

When the ball is snapped, a quarterback has anywhere from three to four seconds to throw the football. If a quarterback can get the football out of his hands and thrown downfield under four seconds without getting sacked, a team's completion percentage is high. The longer a quarterback holds the football, the lower his completion percentage will drop. When facing press coverage, a wide receiver should keep this thought in mind when formulating a plan of attack. In the release phase, a wide receiver has about 1.2 seconds to obtain a release and enter the approach phase of his pass route. Every tenth of a second matters when running a pass route. A wide receiver should use every tenth of a second to his advantage if he wants to obtain a clean release. His internal clock will tell a wide receiver when he needs to present a target for the quarterback to throw to. Maximizing the 1.2 seconds a wide receiver has for his release phase is why it's important to use his speed and quickness to make quick concise movements with his hands and feet.

For a wide receiver to maximize his time during the release phase of his pass route, he should move his body in perfect unison. Every moment is critical during the release phase, and being able to move as quickly and efficiently as possible is essential for a wide receiver. To be efficient in the release phase of his pass route, a wide receiver should make quick, concise, synchronized movements with his hands and feet. When releasing out of his stance against press coverage, a wide receiver doesn't want to take long strides. Instead, he wants to shorten his strides and accentuate his ability to take short, quick steps. At the same time his feet are moving, a wide receiver should use his hands to quickly dismiss a defender's jam technique. Using quick, concise, synchronized movements with his hands and feet, a wide receiver can maximize his efficiency and begin to use his speed to threaten a defender vertically down the field.

When a wide receiver faces press coverage, he should always keep in mind a defender's biggest fear: giving up a touchdown by being beat vertically down the field. Usually, a defender is aligned eight to 10 yards off, but when playing press coverage, he doesn't have a cushion between a wide receiver and himself. The fact that every defender is scared of being beaten vertically down the field gives a wide receiver a huge advantage when facing press coverage. Every time a wide receiver attempts to beat press coverage, he should use his speed and quickness to threaten a defender vertically down the field. The quicker a wide receiver can release vertically upfield, the quicker he'll obtain a clean release. The worst thing that can happen to a wide receiver when facing press coverage is to get flattened out laterally by a defender. If a wide receiver is getting flattened out, he's not properly using his speed and quickness to threaten a defender vertically. Using quick, concise hand and feet movements, a wide receiver should sell to a defender the possibility that he's going to run by him for a touchdown. Properly selling the possibility of being beaten vertically by a wide receiver to a defender will allow a wide receiver to quickly and efficiently obtain a clean release within the 1.2 seconds allotted to him during the release phase.

Aggressive Release Fundamentals

If a wide receiver is going to be able to obtain a clean release from the line of scrimmage, he should be extremely aggressive with his hands and feet. Being aggressive is the fourth key to obtaining a clean release. For a wide receiver to be aggressive during the release phase, he should develop an aggressive mindset that no defender is going to hold him up at the line of scrimmage. Knowing how to use his hands to fight off a defender's jamming technique is also critical. If a wide receiver can learn these different aspects about being aggressive during the release phase, then he'll be able to accomplish the fourth key to obtaining a clean release during the release phase.

For a wide receiver to successfully obtain a release from the line of scrimmage during the release phase of his pass route, he should develop an aggressive mindset. The release phase is the most physical phase of a wide receiver's pass route. During the release phase, a wide receiver should be prepared for a collision between himself and a defender. To win the collision, a wide receiver should develop a physical aggressive attitude. To develop an aggressive attitude, a wide receiver should be aware of how physical the release phase is going to be and what he can expect during the first five yards of his pass route. A wide receiver can expect a defender to try to knock him off the football by using his hands to jam a wide receiver's get-off. A defender's jam technique will be very aggressive and physical. If a wide receiver understands what to expect, then he can prepare himself mentally to be more physical and aggressive than the defender. During the release phase, a wide receiver should attempt to knock a hole in the defender's chest. He should use his hands to violently chop down a defender's hands to win during the release phase. If a wide receiver can knock a hole in the defender's chest and violently chop down his hands, he'll be able to win in the release phase of his pass route by having an aggressive attitude.

During the release phase of his pass route, a wide receiver should learn how to use his hands to become aggressive at the line of scrimmage. A wide receiver never wants a defender's hands to be more aggressive than his hands during the release phase. To accomplish this task, a wide receiver should start by having proper hand placement in his stance. When a defender is aligned head up on a wide receiver in a press coverage position, a wide receiver should always position his hands above a defender's hands (Figure 4-2). If a wide receiver has his hands positioned above a defender's hands, then he'll be in a better position to knock a defender's hands down when the defender attempts to jam him. If a wide receiver keeps his hands low below a defender, then the defender will be in a favorable position to beat a wide receiver's hands and successfully jam a wide receiver.

Figure 4-2. When facing press coverage, a wide receiver should align in his stance with his hand's above a defender's hands.

Once a wide receiver has his hands positioned properly, then he should learn how to use his hands effectively to defeat a defender's jam technique. The two main techniques a wide receiver should use to be aggressive with his hands are the short swim and the punch and rip. At the snap of the football, if a wide receiver is attempting the short swim hand movement, he needs to grab with his outside hand the wrist of a defender's arm to the side he's attempting to release to. After grabbing a defender's wrist, a wide receiver needs to turn the defender's shoulders as close as possible to 90 degrees by pulling down on the defender's wrist. As he pulls the defender's wrist down, a wide receiver needs to shoot his opposite arm to the defender's shoulder, pinning the defender's bicep area. When attempting the short swim, a wide receiver shouldn't swim the opposite arm too high (Figure 4-3). If a wide receiver does attempt a high swim, he'll leave the side of his body exposed for a defender to knock him off course.

The next arm movement a wide receiver should learn is the punch and rip technique. At the snap of the ball, a wide receiver should punch with his outside arm the shoulder of a defender to the side he's attempting to release to. Once a defender's shoulders open from the punch movement, a wide receiver should dip his opposite shoulder under a defender's shoulder pads. As a wide receiver dips his shoulder, he should rip his near arm through the defender's arms to gain a clean release (Figure 4-4). The short swim and the punch and rip can and should be accompanied with aggressive foot movement releases, which are discussed later in this chapter.

Figure 4-3. Short swim technique

Figure 4-4. Punch and rip

Deception Release Fundamentals

The fifth key a wide receiver should accomplish to win during the release phase of his pass route is to be deceptive with his release. If a wide receiver expects to win during the release phase, he should learn to use a variety of releases. A wide receiver can't try to use the same release all the time. If a wide receiver attempts to use the same release repeatedly, he'll find it's very difficult to obtain a release. Using the same release will make a wide receiver predictable. Part of being great during the release phase for a wide receiver is being deceptive. A wide receiver wants to create a difference of opinion about which way he's releasing between himself and a defender. To make this happen, a wide receiver should be armed with an array of different releases he can use during the release phase. It should be noted that in every release discussed, a wide receiver should remember to be aggressive with his hands and use either a short swim or a punch and rip hand motion to win with his release.

Types of Releases

Speed Release

The key to the speed release is, of course, speed. To use the speed release, a wide receiver should have great speed. If a wide receiver with average speed tries the speed release, he'll get cut off by a defender and walled to the sideline. The speed release is the most basic release a wide receiver can use but can only be properly executed by some. At the snap of the football, a wide receiver should step in the direction he intends to release. On his second step, a wide receiver should dip his inside shoulder and try to run by the defender as fast as possible. Once he's cleared the defender, a wide receiver should get back on top or stack a defender as fast as possible (Figure 4-5). Ideally, the speed release should be used on a deep vertical pass route, such as a post route or streak route.

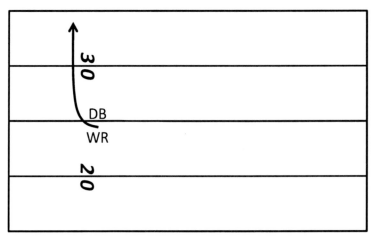

Figure 4-5. When using the speed release, a wide receiver will beat a defender as quickly as possible with great speed. After beating the defender, a wide receiver should then stack on top of him as fast as possible.

Single Move Release

The single move release requires a wide receiver to make one decisive move, then work into his release. The decisive move can be a head fake, a hard stick plant off the foot, or a shoulder fake. Learning to use a single move release creates a great foundation for a wide receiver to build off and use more intricate releases. When a wide receiver decides to use a single move release, he should make sure the move he chooses to use is decisive and distinct. The first thing a wide receiver should do when using a single move release is come to balance. At the snap of the football, a wide receiver's first step should bring his feet parallel to each other and shoulder-width apart. Bringing his feet to a balanced position will let a wide receiver use a single move release to either his inside or outside. Coming to balance will keep a defender guessing on whether a wide receiver is releasing inside. If a wide receiver decides to use a head fake, he should come to balance, then snap his head in the opposite direction he intends to run. The head-snapping movement is intended to get a defender to turn his hips in the opposite direction a wide receiver is actually releasing.

Ideally, when using a single move release, a wide receiver should come to balance, then use a hard stick plant as his single move release. If a wide receiver wants to release to the inside of a defender, then he should stick-plant off his outside foot. If he wants to release to the outside, then he should stick-plant off his inside foot. When attempting a stick plant, a wide receiver needs to make sure he plants his foot outside his body's framework. The stick plant is an aggressive movement that when used properly is designed to get a defender in press coverage to jump the opposite way a wide receiver intends to release (Figure 4-6).

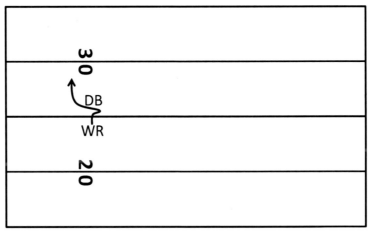

Figure 4-6. The single move release requires a wide receiver to use either a head fake or a stick plant to get a defender to open his hips in the opposite direction a wide receiver intends to release. After coming to balance, a wide receiver can use either a head fake, a stick plant, or both.

Footfire Release

A footfire release is designed to freeze a defender by attacking his leverage with short, choppy steps and then finishing with a stick plant. As a wide receiver releases at the snap of the football, he should use short, quick, choppy steps to attack a defender's leverage. After attacking a defender's leverage, a wide receiver should finish his footfire by using a stick plant or head to get a defender to open up in the opposite direction he intends to release. A footfire release should be used when a wide receiver is unsure if a defender is playing with inside or outside leverage. The footfire action at the line of scrimmage will give a wide receiver the extra time needed to see how a defender is playing him. The footfire action will force a defender onto his heels and into his backpedal, which will give away how he's trying to defend a wide receiver. The footfire release should be incorporated with a single move release to ensure a wide receiver is going to win during the release phase (Figure 4-7).

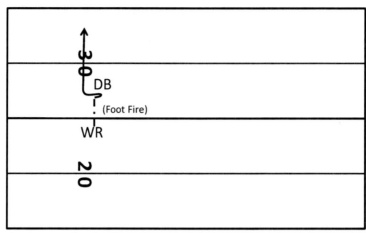

Figure 4-7. The footfire release requires a wide receiver to attack a defender's leverage with short, quick, choppy steps. A footfire release should be accompanied with a single move release.

Double Move Release

A double move release is a great away for a wide receiver to change up the tendencies of his releases. Before a wide receiver attempts a double move release, he should first master the single move release. Two types of double move releases exist:

- An in-out-in, which should be used when a wide receiver is attempting an inside release
- An out-in-out, which should be used when a wide receiver is attempting an outside release

These releases use the same technique and footwork. The only difference is their aim points. One goes inside and the other goes outside. At the snap of the football, the first thing a wide receiver should do is step with the foot that's farthest back in his stance and come to balance. After coming to balance, a wide receiver can then attempt an in-out-in release if he needs to release to the inside of a defender or an out-in-out release if he needs to release to the outside. For this example, an in-out-in release will be explained. After coming to balance, a wide receiver should take a short, quick step with his inside foot. After stepping with the inside foot, a wide receiver should quickly transition to a short, quick step with his outside foot. Stick-planting off his outside foot, a wide receiver should transition back to his inside foot. Using aggressive hand and arm movement techniques, a wide receiver should then have created enough movement to successfully release past a pressed defender by using an in-out-in release (Figure 4-8).

To use an out-in-out release, a wide receiver should first come to balance. After coming to balance, a wide receiver should take a short, quick step with his outside foot. After stepping with the outside foot, a wide receiver should quickly transition to a short, quick step with his inside foot. Stick-planting off his inside foot, a wide receiver should transition back to his outside foot. This movement will allow a wide receiver to successfully use an out-in-out release to win at the line of scrimmage during the release phase of his pass route (Figure 4-9).

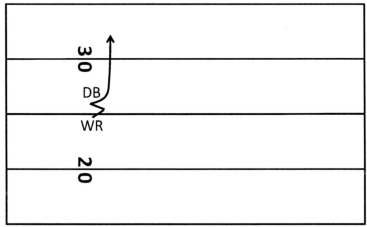

Figure 4-8. To use an in-out-in release, a wide receiver should first come to balance, then step quickly with his inside foot. After stepping with his inside foot, a wide receiver should use a stick plant off his outside foot to propel him back to his inside foot and past the pressed defender.

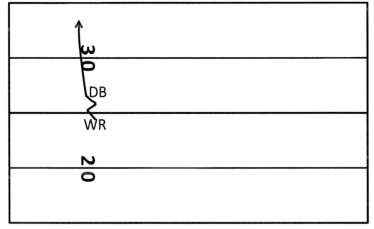

Figure 4-9. To use an out-in-out release, a wide receiver should flip his footwork, causing him to step with the outside foot first after coming to balance.

Hard Inside Release

The hard inside release is designed to get a pressed defender to move laterally with a wide receiver to gain the space needed to properly release from the line of scrimmage. The hard inside release should be used when a defender is playing with inside leverage and a wide receiver wants to release to the outside of a defender. The hard inside release is a great way for a wide receiver to create extra space to run a pass route that's near the sideline or for a slot receiver to create extra space to run an outward-breaking pass route, such as a corner route or an out route.

At the snap of the football, a wide receiver should attack a defender's inside leverage by moving him laterally to the inside. To move the defender laterally, a wide receiver should take at least three quick steps laterally down the line of scrimmage. The quick lateral steps will cause a pressed defender to move inside with a wide receiver laterally down the line of scrimmage. After taking at least three steps lateral, a wide receiver should stick-plant off his inside foot by using aggressive hand and arm movements, then work to stack a defender as quickly as possible. The lateral hard inside release puts a lot of pressure on a defender's inside leverage, which will cause him to be out of position when he's trying to cover an outward breaking pass route (Figure 4-10).

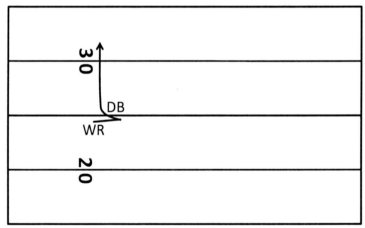

Figure 4-10. Using a hard inside release, a wide receiver should attack a defender's inside leverage with at least three lateral quick steps. After moving the defender lateral, a wide receiver should stick-plant off his inside foot and work to stack a defender.

Widen and Slip Release

The widen and slip release uses the same principles as the hard inside release. But now, instead of releasing to the outside of a defender like a hard inside release, the widen and slip allows a wide receiver to release to the defender's inside. At the snap of the football, a wide receiver should take at least three quick steps laterally, attacking a defender's outside leverage. After widening the defender, a wide receiver should then stick-plant off his outside foot and use aggressive hand and arm movements to stack a defender as quickly as possible (Figure 4-11). The widen and slip release can be very useful against a zone defender who's responsible for the flat; the widening lateral steps will cause the flat defender to widen with a wide receiver, giving a him extra space to run an inward-breaking pass route.

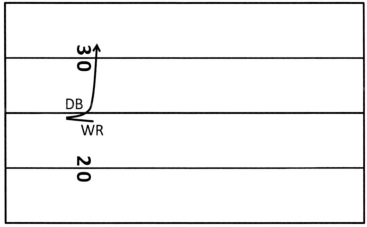

Figure 4-11. Using the widen and slip release, a wide receiver should take three quick steps laterally, attacking a defender's outside leverage. After widening the defender, a wide receiver should then stick-plant off his outside foot and work to stack the defender as quickly as possible.

Release Drills

Drill #1: Partner Releases

Partner releases are designed for a wide receiver to get a lot of repetitions by working his releases in a short period of time (Figure 4-12). Each wide receiver aligns across from a partner. The partner is representing a pressed defender who the wide receiver should work a release against. At the snap of the football, a wide receiver works a release against the pressed defender. Coaches can start by having the wide receivers work a single move release, then work a footfire and go double move release hard inside, and then a widen and slip release. This drill is easy to execute and very time efficient, especially for coaches who are dealing with a large group of wide receivers.

Coaching Points

- The wide receiver shouldn't take any false steps.
- His eyes should be inside, watching for ball movement.
- The wide receiver should be physical and aggressive with his hands and arms.
- He should be patient (overexaggerating his release).
- He should stay low and not expose his pads to a defender.
- Defenders should be physical, making their partners work hard to gain a release.
- The wide receiver should stack the defender as quickly as possible.

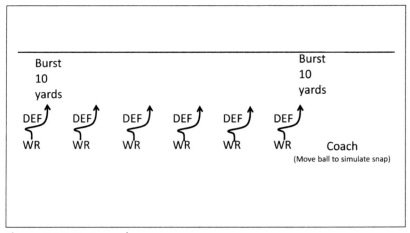

Figure 4-12. Partner releases

Drill #2: Bag Release

The bag release drill is another drill designed for a group of wide receivers to get a lot of repetitions in a short period of time (Figure 4-13). If a team has a pop-up dummy, then coaches can use the pop-up dummy for the wide receivers to work on their release phase. If a team doesn't have a pop-up dummy, then the coach can hold a bag and have his wide receivers work a release off the bag. Coaches can start by having the wide receivers work a single move release, then work a footfire and go double move release hard inside, and then a widen and slip release. This drill is easy to execute and very time efficient, especially for coaches who are dealing with a large group of wide receivers. Coaches should move the bag to different positions to simulate different releases.

Coaching Points

- The wide receiver shouldn't take any false steps.
- His eyes should be inside, watching for ball movement.
- The wide receiver should be physical and aggressive with his hands and arms.
- He should be patient (overexaggerating his release).
- He should stay low and not expose his pads to a defender.
- Defenders should be physical, making their partners work hard to gain a release.
- The wide receiver should stack the defender as quickly as possible.

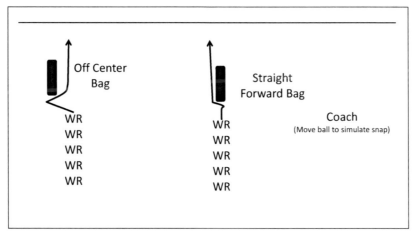

Figure 4-13. Bag release drills

Drill #3: Hand-to-Hand Combat

Like the other drills mentioned so far, the hand-to-hand combat drill is a great way to get a lot of repetitions in a short period of time (Figure 4-14). For this drill, each wide receiver needs a partner align one-half yards across from him. Each set of partners will work its punch and rip and short swim techniques. Also, partners will work on batting away the defender's hands. The partner designated as the wide receiver will jog in place. When the defender shoots his hands to attempt to jam the wide receiver, the wide receiver should bat the defender's hands down. The coach should have everyone work a punch and rip first, followed by a short swim, then work an inside hand batdown. After taking reps by using each hand movement, the partners switch and repeat.

Coaching Points

- The wide receiver should anticipate the defender's hand movements and be prepared for contact.
- He should be physical and aggressive with his hands and arms.
- He should beat the defender's hands and knock them down.
- He shouldn't swim high or expose his body.
- He should step through the defender's hip after beating his hands.

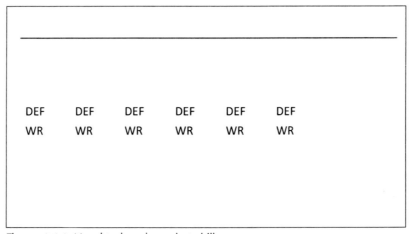

Figure 4-14. Hand-to-hand combat drill

Drill #4: Jam vs. Defensive Backs

The jam drill is an ultracompetitive drill that pits the wide receiver group against the defensive back group (Figure 4-15). The jam drill is designed for a wide receiver to work a release against the defender in a 5x5 square. If a wide receiver steps out-of-bounds or is jammed out-of-bounds by a defender, the defense wins the drill. If a wide receiver wins his release and finishes through the cones, the offense wins. It's the coach's job to tell his wide receivers which route they should run. This will determine if a wide receiver takes an inside or an outside release. For example, if the coach told a wide receiver he's running a fade pass route, the wide receiver would want to take an outside release.

Coaching Points

- The wide receiver shouldn't take any false steps.
- His eyes should be inside, watching for ball movement.
- The wide receiver should be physical and aggressive with his hands and arms.
- He should be patient (overexaggerating his release).
- He should stay low and not expose his pads to a defender.
- He should stack the defender as quickly as possible.

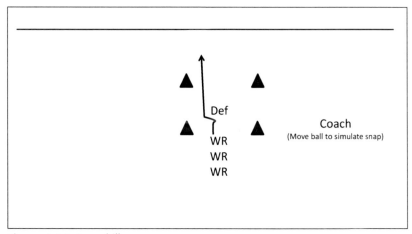

Figure 4-15. Jam drill

Drill #5: Fade vs. Defensive Backs

The fade drill is another way to work on obtaining a sound release from the line of scrimmage for a wide receiver (Figure 4-16). Like the jam drill, this drill is very competitive and is a great way to compete against the defensive backs in practice. Also, the fade drill is a great way for the quarterbacks and wide receivers to work on their pass timing when throwing the fade pass route. At the snap of the football, a wide receiver needs to work a release against the defender and obtain a clean outside release. After clearing the defender, a wide receiver should then work to stack the defender as quick as possible and hold space from the sideline to have enough room to catch the football.

Coaching Points

- The wide receiver shouldn't take any false steps.
- His eyes should be inside, watching for ball movement.
- The wide receiver should be physical and aggressive with his hands and arms.
- He should be patient (overexaggerating his release).
- He should stay low and not expose his pads to a defender.
- He should stack the defender as quickly as possible.
- He should hold space away from the sideline.

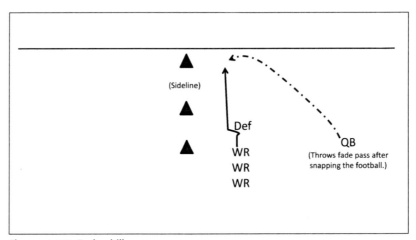

Figure 4-16. Fade drill

5

Wide Receiver Route Running

Running pass route patterns is a skill that can takes year to develop. Great pass route runners aren't born; they're made through hours of practice on the field and by studying film. A wide receiver may have such physical attributes as great speed, size, or quickness that helps him succeed on the football field. However, having such physical attributes doesn't guarantee that a wide receiver is going to be a great pass route runner. Such physical attributes can help a wide receiver become a great pass route runner, but to truly be great at running pass routes, a wide receiver should have a complete and thorough understanding of the inner workings of his team's passing game, the defense's scheme he sees in front of him, the defensive player's leverage, and how best to exploit the defense with his pass route pattern. This chapter will focus on the basic fundamentals and techniques it takes for a wide receiver to become a great pass route runner.

To be a great pass route runner, a wide receiver should fully understand what he's trying to accomplish with his assigned pass route and what his teammates are trying to accomplish with their routes. Every time a wide receiver runs a pass route, he should have a plan and a purpose for how he's going to accomplish his assigned pass route. If a slot wide receiver's assigned pass route is to run a three-step slant route, aiming for the outside linebacker's inside shoulder, he should understand why he's aiming for the outside linebacker's inside shoulder. Also, the slot receiver should understand how he's going to accomplish his assigned task. To fully understand his job, a wide receiver has to know what the other wide receivers, tight ends, and running backs are doing on every play. For a passing game to be successful, every individual route of a pass pattern should work in perfect unison with each other and be in sync with the quarterback.

Watching a great passing team is like watching a surgeon performing surgery with perfect precision. Every wide receiver, tight end, or running back that's part of the assigned pass pattern should be in sync with each other and the quarterback. If everybody is in sync and on the same page, then the quarterback will know precisely where each wide receiver is going to break off his pass route. This will enable the quarterback to deliver the football to his wide receivers with great timing. To gain this sense of unison, a wide receiver should first understand and master the basic fundamentals and techniques it takes to become a great pass route runner.

Approach Phase Fundamentals

First and foremost, a wide receiver's success on any play depends on having a great stance and start off the line of scrimmage. If a wide receiver is facing press coverage with a defender lined up directly over the top of him, his success will hinge on obtaining a great release off the line of scrimmage. After achieving a great stance, start, and release, a wide receiver enters into the next phase of his pass route pattern: the approach phase. The approach, or stem, is the technique used by a wide receiver between five yards and 18 yards down the field or until a wide receiver reaches the breakpoint of his pass route. A wide receiver has two goals he should try to accomplish to win the approach phase of his pass route. First, he should use the approach phase to gain leverage on a defender. Second, he should reduce the distance between himself and a defender as quickly as possible. Closing the distance between a defender and a wide receiver is called *reducing a defender's cushion*. A wide receiver wants to reduce a defender's cushion as quickly as possible. The quicker a wide receiver closes a defender's cushion, the faster a defender will open up his hips and transition from his backpedal into a full-blown sprint. If a wide receiver can accomplish the two goals of the approach phase, then he'll be in position to win his pass route pattern.

Proper Eye Placement Approach Phase Fundamentals

As a wide receiver releases off the line of scrimmage, his eyes need to be up and analyzing the defense's coverage. The information gathered from his pre-snap analysis of the defense's alignment and from his first three steps off the line of scrimmage should give a wide receiver the information needed to identify the defense's coverage. Properly indentifying the defense's coverage will make it easier for a wide receiver to properly execute his job during the approach phase of his pass route.

When a wide receiver enters the approach phase of his pass route, he should make certain he utilizes proper eye placement fundamentals. The approach phase lasts from five yards to 18 yards or to the breakpoint of a wide receiver's pass route. During this phase, a wide receiver's head and eyes need to be up looking directly at the eyes of the defensive back who's trying to cover him. Having his head and eyes up looking at the defender can further provide a wide receiver with the information needed to execute his pass route. While looking at the defense back's eyes, a wide receiver needs to be analyzing the defender's posture and leverage. During the approach phase, a wide receiver should ask himself: "How is this defender trying to cover me? What move or fake is going to get me open? Is a move or fake even needed to beat the defender?" These questions can be answered by using the information gathered during his pre-snap scan, during his release phase, and by using proper eye placement fundamentals during the approach phase.

Throughout the approach phase, a wide receiver should also use his eyes to be aware of the defenders around him. A wide receiver should use his peripheral vision to see and feel the defenders around him. By using his peripheral vision, a wide receiver can prepare and plan to maneuver around a defender who might be attempting to reroute him off his pass route. A wide receiver should also use his peripheral vision to further identify the defense's coverage during the approach phase. Using his peripheral vision, a wide receiver will be able to recognize any late secondary rotations and movement. Developing great peripheral vision throughout the approach phase will give a wide receiver an essential tool necessary to run a successful pass route.

Proper Arm and Elbow Approach Phase Fundamentals

When entering the approach phase of a pass route, a wide receiver should use proper arm and elbow techniques and fundamentals. After obtaining a get-off and release from the line of scrimmage, a wide receiver should be able to produce proper sprint running form as quickly as possible. The arm and elbow should be bent at a 90-degree angle. The elbows should swing as close to the body as possible and in a straight line. The swinging action of a wide receiver's elbows and arms should never cross his body. Swinging the arms across the body is detrimental to a wide receiver's running form and will slow him down. The proper arm swing action is called a *wide receiver's elbow jam*. When using great elbow jam form, a wide receiver should never drop his arms below waist level and should never swing across the body, as shown in Figure 5-1. In the approach phase of his pass route, a wide receiver can make himself appear faster than he really is by quickening his elbow jam. The quickening of his elbow jam will also cause a wide receiver's legs to speed up, which should increase his speed over time. In addition, it could give off the illusion to a defender that a wide receiver is gaining speed.

During the approach phase, a wide receiver should be prepared to use his arms and hands to help him avoid being rerouted. The chance of a wide receiver being rerouted by a defender is highest during the approach phase. As a wide receiver enters the approach phase, it's essential that his arms don't drop below waist level. A wide receiver should keep his arms up to execute great elbow jam and in case he has to use his arms to avoid being rerouted. If a defender comes to reroute a wide receiver,

Figure 5-1. Elbow jam fundamentals

he shouldn't allow a defender to knock him off his pass route. A wide receiver should always be prepared to knock a defender's hands down whenever a defender attempts to reroute him. A common way to accomplish this task is for a wide receiver to use the hammer down technique, as shown in Figure 5-2. In the hammer down technique, a wide receiver uses his closest hand and arm to knock down the hand of the defender who's trying to reroute him. A wide receiver should use his near hand and arm like a hammer and strike down on the defender's arm. This will knock the defender's arm away so the defender can't reroute a wide receiver.

Another technique a wide receiver can use is the club and rip technique. In the club and rip technique, a wide receiver will club the defender with his outside arm and rip through him with his inside arm. When ripping through the defender, a wide receiver shouldn't confuse the rip movement with a swim technique. If a wide receiver rips his inside hand through the defender too high, like in a swim move, he'll expose the side of his torso. Exposing the side of his torso will give the defender a huge target to physically knock a wide receiver off his pass route.

Once a wide receiver has defeated a reroute technique, it's essential he gets right back on track to continue running his pass route. A wide receiver should never let a

Figure 5-2. Hammer down technique

defender reroute him off his pass route. In addition, when defeating a reroute technique by a defender, a wide receiver should never let a defender push him into his pass route break. A precision break and cut should always be made even if a wide receiver has had to fend off a defender's reroute attempt.

Leverage Approach Phase Fundamentals

As a wide receiver enters into the approach phase of his pass route, he should work to gain the proper leverage on the defense player covering him needed to run his pass route successfully. For a wide receiver to gain the proper leverage needed to run his pass route, he needs to understand what it is he's trying to accomplish with his pass route and how proper leverage impacts his pass route. Gaining leverage on a defender can be the difference between an incompletion and a completion. When running pass routes, a wide receiver should always be aware of how a defender is trying to cover him. A wide receiver should also know how to adjust each of his pass routes to defeat the different types of leverages and coverages an opponent will run. For any pass route to be successful, a wide receiver should gain proper leverage on a defender. This is true whether a wide receiver needs to gain inside leverage or outside leverage or, on some pass routes, needs to get to the center of a defender's body which, is called *gaining 50/50 leverage*.

If a wide receiver is running an inward breaking route, such as a slant or dig pass route, and a defender is playing him with outside leverage, the wide receiver can then run his pass route normally as long as he maintains inside leverage on the defender. Maintaining leverage requires a wide receiver to use a leverage stem. Using a leverage stem tells a wide receiver that he already has the defender beat with his initial alignment. Also, this tells him he can't give up any leverage that he's already won from the defender during the execution of his pass route. For example, this would be true if a wide receiver is running a three-step slant pass route and the defender has outside leverage on him. A wide receiver can then use a leverage stem and take three steps vertically upfield, plant off his outside foot, and break off his route. This allows him to maintain inside leverage on the defender and win his pass route battle. If the defender is playing him with inside leverage, a wide receiver should then adjust his thinking when attempting to run the same three-step slant route.

When attacking a defender with inside leverage, a wide receiver should attack the defender's leverage by stemming his pass route at the defender to negate leverage. Stemming his pass route at the defender means a wide receiver should attack the defender's leverage during his approach phase of the pass route (Figure 5-3). Attacking a defender's leverage means a wide receiver can't just release straight upfield, take three steps, and then break his route in. If a wide receiver does this, when the football is thrown, the defender will have the inside track to the football and have a better chance to break the pass up or make an interception. Instead, a wide receiver should come off the football by using a technique called a *weave stem*. The weave stem tells a wide receiver to weave his pass route to the defender's inside shoulder by the time he reaches his breakpoint for his pass route. Using the weave stem will allow a wide receiver to attack the defender's inside shoulder and will help him negate the defender's leverage. If a wide receiver uses the weave stem correctly and works to a defender's inside shoulder, then he'll have positioned himself between the defender

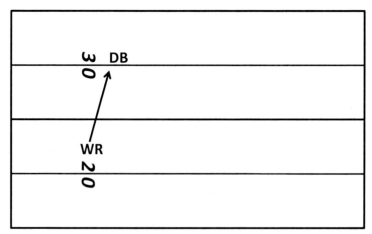

Figure 5-3. The wide receiver uses a weave stem to gain leverage.

and the football when running his three-step slant route. The weave stem technique should always be used by a wide receiver to gain inside leverage on a defender during the approach phase of his pass route.

The same idea of using a weave stem applies for a wide receiver when he's trying to gain outside leverage on a defender. If a wide receiver is trying to gain outside leverage on a defender, he should still use his weave stem technique to gain outside leverage on the defender covering him. A wide receiver should attack the defender's outside shoulder with his weave stem technique throughout his approach phase. If he properly uses the weave stem technique upon reaching his breakpoint, a wide receiver will have advantageous leverage on the defender trying to cover him.

Not all pass routes require a wide receiver to gain inside or outside leverage on a defender during the approach phase. In many cases, a wide receiver should work to get to the middle of a defender's body. Getting to the middle of a defender's body is called gaining 50/50 leverage with the defender (Figure 5-4). Gaining 50/50 leverage is a very advantageous position for a wide receiver to be in. Gaining 50/50 leverage doesn't give away the direction of his pass route break to a defender. By getting into a position where he has 50/50 leverage, a wide receiver can now break his pass route off inside, outside, vertically, or back to the football, giving him a technique called *gaining the spoke of the wheel* (Figure 5-5).

When a wide receiver has achieved the spoke of the wheel, a defender now has to be prepared for a wide receiver to break in any direction. The spoke of the wheel is achieved by a wide receiver gaining 50/50 leverage on a defender. Gaining 50/50 leverage can make a wide receiver very unpredictable to a defender. Having 50/50 leverage is also a good way for a wide receiver to deviate from normal pass route running tendencies. Again, if a wide receiver is running a three-step slant pass route,

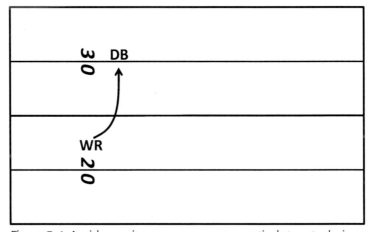

Figure 5-4. A wide receiver uses a weave or vertical stem technique to gain 50/50 leverage.

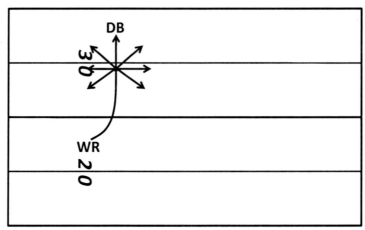

Figure 5-5. Spoke of the wheel

the first time he runs the pass route, he might weave-stem the defender to gain inside leverage before he breaks off his pass route. The next time he runs a slant pass route, he might weave-stem a defender to gain inside leverage before he breaks off his pass route. Adding subtle differences to individual pass routes will make a wide receiver unpredictable and hard for a defender to cover him. Achieving 50/50 leverage and the spoke of the wheel are tools a wide receiver has in his arsenal to use during the approach phase of his pass route.

Influencing Approach Phase Fundamentals

It's sometimes difficult for a wide receiver to gain proper leverage on a defender. When a wide receiver can't gain proper leverage, he should then try to influence the defender away from the direction in which he's going to break off his pass route. When trying to influence a defender, a wide receiver has a distinct advantage over the defender who's trying to cover him. The advantage is that a wide receiver knows exactly what pass route he's assigned to run. Also, he knows in which direction and at what depth he's going to break off his pass route. The defender doesn't know what pass route a wide receiver is going to run and in what direction or at what depth a wide receiver is going to break off his pass route. To successfully influence a defender, a wide receiver should use a variety of techniques. He should sell a defender on the idea he's running a vertical pass route. He should use head, shoulder, and hip fakes to trick a defender into thinking he's breaking off his pass route in a different direction than he actually is. To successfully influence a defender, a wide receiver should use one or a variety of different techniques to successfully influence a defender away from the direction he's running is pass route.

An advantage a wide receiver should always maintain over a defender is the threat of running a deep vertical pass route, such as a streak pass route or a post route. A wide receiver should always keep this advantage in mind when he's running a pass route.

Every defender in football is scared of being beat deep by a wide receiver. Because of this, a wide receiver should use a vertical stem technique when running pass routes. Every time a wide receiver runs a pass route, he should threaten a defender deep with a vertical stem. During the approach phase of his pass route, a wide receiver should always sell the idea that he's running a vertical pass route to a defender. Selling the idea that he's going deep will keep a defender on his heels and cause him to turn and run earlier out of his backpedal. To sell the idea of a deep pass route, a wide receiver should always run every pass route as if he's going deep down the field. Even if a wide receiver is really running a six-yard hitch pass route, a wide receiver can create more separation between him and the defender by selling a vertical deep pass route than he can if he's running at a slower speed. If sold properly, using a vertical stem will always make a defender think a wide receiver is going to beat the defender down the field and will force the defender to open his hips too early. If a wide receiver can get a defender to open his hips, then he's successfully sold the threat of going deep down the field and will give himself a better chance to execute the pass route he's actually running.

Faking Approach Phase Fundamentals

Sometimes, as a wide receiver is running his pass route, he can't gain proper leverage on a defender by simply stemming his pass route to the defender's inside or outside shoulder. When a wide receiver can't gain leverage, he should influence the defender away from the direction he's running his pass route. Using head, shoulder, and hip fakes can help a wide receiver properly influence a defender away from the point at which he's going to break off his pass route. Fakes are designed to create an illusion for the defender about where a wide receiver is actually going.

For a wide receiver to successfully use a fake to influence a defender, he should learn how to use his hips to his advantage. Hip fakes are the key to any combination of fakes a wide receiver can use when running a pass route. Learning to turn his hips away from where a wide receiver is attempting to break off his pass route will help create an illusion for the defender about where a wide receiver is breaking off his pass route. When attempting a hip fake, a wide receiver should turn his hips in the opposite direction from where he's going to break off his pass route. Turning the hips opposite of where he's breaking off his pass route will cause a defender to turn his hips to the direction in which a faking wide receiver is turning his hips. Once a wide receiver has caused a defender to turn his hips in the opposite direction from which he intends to break off his pass route, a wide receiver will know he's successfully influenced the defender and has gained the leverage needed to successfully execute his pass route.

When attempting to use a fake, a wide receiver should always remember to use his head and eyes to his advantage. A wide receiver's head and eyes are great tools of deception when trying to influence a defender. A wide receiver can use quick head and shoulder fakes to influence a defender away from the direction he's breaking off his pass route. When attempting a head fake, a wide receiver should incorporate a head fake with a hip fake. When a wide receiver turns his hips away from the direction he's intending to run his pass route, he can also snap his head in the same direction he performing his hip fake. In combination with a hip fake, the head snapping action is a great way to influence a defender away from where a wide receiver is intending to break off his pass route. A wide receiver should also remember to look a defender in the eye while he's attempting to influence the defender. Looking a defender in the eye while a wide receiver is performing a fake is essential for a wide receiver to properly execute his fake and influence the defender.

When a wide receiver uses a fake to influence a defender during his pass route, he should always remember to not overdo his fake. Game situations require less faking than practice situations due to a defender's increased fear of being beaten deep. A good rule for a wide receiver is to limit himself to one or two fakes per pass route. It should also be noted that a wide receiver can and should use faking techniques throughout his final breakpoint, not just in the approach phase. More faking techniques will be discussed in the breakpoint fundamentals section of this chapter.

Breakpoint Fundamentals

Once a wide receiver has finished his approach and has reached the desired depth of his pass route, he should now break off his pass route. Understanding proper breakpoint fundamentals and techniques is essential for a wide receiver to become a great pass route runner. The objective of the breakpoint is for a wide receiver to gain distance from a defender. Gaining distance between a wide receiver and a defender is called *creating separation*. A wide receiver can have great approach phase fundamentals, but if he doesn't execute great technique at his breakpoint, he'll never gain the separation needed to successfully catch a pass against a defender. To create separation at his breakpoint, a wide receiver should make his final break at full speed. He should keep a low center of gravity and make precision cuts. If a wide receiver does all three of these concepts, he'll then create the separation needed against a defender to defeat his coverage.

Speed and Acceleration Breakpoint Fundamentals

When running any pass route, a wide receiver should run the assigned pass route at full speed to execute the pass route properly. As a wide receiver leaves the approach phase of his pass route and enters the breakpoint phase, he should maintain the speed he's gained during the approach phase. He should then continue to maintain such a speed throughout the breakpoint phase. Maintaining full speed throughout the breakpoint phase isn't an easy task for a wide receiver to accomplish. A great wide receiver can accelerate in and out of his breakpoint at or near full speed every time he runs a pass route. Accelerating out of his breakpoint at full speed will create separation between a wide receiver and a defender. To accomplish the task of accelerating full speed out of his breakpoint, a wide receiver should be sure to execute great arm swing technique.

To accelerate out of his breakpoint, a wide receiver should increase the speed of his arm swing, called his *elbow jam*. Maintaining speed and accelerating out of his breakpoint hinges on how fast a wide receiver can accelerate his elbow jam. When a wide receiver reaches his breakpoint, his elbow jam should speed up. The faster his elbow jam increases, the faster his feet are going to move, which will increase the speed with which a wide receiver exits from his breakpoint. Without increasing the speed of his elbow jam throughout the breakpoint phase of his pass route, a wide receiver can't expect to accelerate efficiently out of his breakpoint.

Once a wide receiver understands the importance of increasing the speed of his elbow jam, he'll now be able to properly speed up his feet at his breakpoint. It's essential for a wide receiver's feet to speed up with his elbow jam throughout his breakpoint. To maintain speed during the breakpoint phase, a wide receiver should make sure he makes his break with the proper plant foot. A wide receiver's plant foot is the foot he's attempting to cut off during the breakpoint phase. The plant foot will be a wide receiver's inside foot if he's running an outward-breaking pass route, such as an out route. If a wide receiver is running an inward-breaking pass route, such as a post route, his outside foot will be his plant foot. When entering the breakpoint phase, a wide receiver should always make sure his plant foot is firmly positioned underneath his hip to create explosiveness throughout his breakpoint. If the plant foot is positioned outside the hip, a wide receiver's center of gravity will be thrown off, which will cause a wide receiver to not make his breakpoint at full speed. If the plant foot is positioned correctly, a wide receiver will then be able to make his break at full speed.

Center of Gravity Breakpoint Fundamentals

For a wide receiver to maximize the potential of his breakpoint fundamentals, he should keep a low center of gravity when he's making cuts and breaks. For a wide receiver to develop proper breakpoint fundamentals, he should learn his center of gravity techniques from the ground up. A wide receiver's center of gravity progression needs to start with his feet and knees. The progression then moves to his hips. Finally, it progresses to his shoulders and head.

When a wide receiver reaches his final breakpoint, he should use his plant foot to start the breakpoint phase. As a wide receiver pushes off his plant foot, his feet need to be spread at least shoulder-width apart to maintain proper balance. If a wide receiver's feet are too narrow, his whole center of gravity and balance will be too narrow and it will be hard for him to cut at full speed. A wide receiver's feet are essentially the key to the entire breakpoint. Proper footwork will put his entire body in position to have a low center of gravity throughout the entire breakpoint phase. Once a wide receiver understands where to place his feet, he can then focus on attaining the proper knee bend to make a successful cut into his pass route.

When a wide receiver makes a cut, he needs to make sure his knees are bent. Bending the knees will allow a wide receiver to sink his hips during his breakpoint.

Sinking the hips is essential for a wide receiver to achieve a low center of gravity. When a wide receiver sinks his hips, it naturally causes the upper body to want to sink with him. To properly position his upper body in the breakpoint phase, a wide receiver should keep his feet spread, bend his knees, and sink his hips as he's making a cut (Figure 5-6).

Once the lower half of a wide receiver's body has achieved proper center of gravity fundamentals, his upper body will be in position to follow the lower half's lead. Following the sinking of his hips, a wide receiver should lower his shoulder plane and position his shoulders so they're aligned over his knees. This will cause his knees to align over his toes. For a wide receiver to have a proper center of gravity, his shoulders should be lowered to where they're aligned over the knees. Not lowering his shoulder plane will cause a wide receiver to be too high throughout his breakpoint phase. High shoulder plane action throughout the breakpoint phase will tip off a defender that a wide receiver is slowing down and preparing to enter his breakpoint phase. A wide receiver can't ever expect to run a pass route at full speed if his shoulder plane is high throughout his breakpoint. Having a low shoulder plane—accompanied with the acceleration of his arms—will give off the illusion to a defender that a wide receiver is still accelerating when in actuality he's entering his breakpoint phase.

Understanding how to achieve a low center of gravity will allow a wide receiver to have excellent body control throughout his breakpoint phase. Having excellent body control will ensure that a wide receiver is running efficient pass routes. For a wide

Figure 5-6. Proper low center of gravity techniques

receiver to have excellent body control throughout his breakpoint phase, he should combine the movement of his entire body. In one motion, he enters his breakpoint, his feet should be spread, his knees should be bent, and his hips should sink, which will allow the shoulder plane to be lowered and positioned over his knees (Figure 5-7). If all these different body parts are moved in perfect unison, a wide receiver will be able to efficiently enter and exit his breakpoint phase as fast as possible and with great body control.

Figure 5-7. Proper breakpoint phase technique

Precision Cuts Breakpoint Fundamentals

The third part of a wide receiver's breakpoint phase that he should master is understanding how to make precision cuts. A wide receiver can be great in his approach phase, run pass routes full speed, and play with great center of gravity. However, if he can't make a precision cut, he's not going to be able to maximize his potential as a pass route runner. Making precision cuts can be the difference between an incompletion and a completion. If a wide receiver rounds out of a breakpoint, he might give a defender the space he needs to break up a pass or even make an interception. To make precision cuts when running his pass route, a wide receiver should learn how to step on a defender's toes before he breaks his pass route off and how to use his plant foot to make precision cuts, called *sticking* a pass route. Once a wide receiver understands how to step on a defender's toes and how to stick a pass route, he'll be ready to use a variety of different breakpoint angles needed to execute all his pass route assignments.

As a wide receiver exits the approach phase and enters the breakpoint phase of his pass route, he should try to break off his pass route as close to a defender as possible. It should be noted that this might not be possible for a wide receiver on all his pass routes, especially if a wide receiver is running a timing pattern, such as a seven-step post. Breaking off a pass route as close to a defender as possible is called *stepping on a defender's toes*. By stepping on a defender's toes, a wide receiver can put a defender on his heels as he breaks off his pass route. Putting a defender on his heels will reduce the defender to a trail position as he attempts to close on a wide receiver's pass route. As a wide receiver steps on a defender's toes, he should also lean into the defender's leverage. Leaning into a defender as a wide receiver breaks off his route will create extra separation between a wide receiver and a defender during his breakpoint phase. Once a wide receiver is as close to a defender as possible and has stepped on the defender's toes and leaned into a defender's leverage, he should then stick the defender with his plant foot to start breaking into his pass route (Figure 5-8).

Sticking his pass route is essential for a wide receiver to run a great pass route. As a wide receiver reaches the breakpoint assigned for his pass route, he should stick his plant foot in the ground to make a precision cut. As a wide receiver attempts a stick, his toe should be planted in the ground and be used as leverage for him to push off the planted toe, propelling a wide receiver into a sharp precision cut. As a wide receiver is attempting a stick his pass route, he needs to throw his opposite elbow from the plant

Figure 5-8. Proper technique for stepping on toes and a body lean into leverage prior to sticking a defender

foot in the direction in which he intends to go. Throwing the opposite elbow of the plant foot will allow a wide receiver to make a precision power step with the opposite foot of his plant foot. The power step is the second step a wide receiver should take after sticking his pass route. The power step will lead a wide receiver into his pass route. If a wide receiver properly executes a stick technique during his pass route, a defender will have to freeze for an instant before he can determine in which direction a wide receiver is cutting. When sticking a defender, a wide receiver shouldn't chop his feet or come to balance before cutting. This will only tip off to a defender that a wide receiver is entering his breakpoint phase. A wide receiver should only chop his feet when the field is wet. Chopping the feet on a wet playing field is necessary for a wide receiver to stay on the balls of his feet throughout the breakpoint phase. When the playing field is in good condition, a wide receiver should always stick his pass route, making a one-step precision cut (Figure 5-9).

For a wide receiver to make a sharp precision cut during his breakpoint phase. A wide receiver should be able to combine all three aspects of breakpoint fundamentals into one precision body movement. A wide receiver should enter the breakpoint phase full speed. He should lower his center of gravity, stepping on a defender's toes and sticking the defender away from the direction in which he intends to break off his pass route. If a wide receiver accomplishes all these things, he'll make a precision cut, creating separation from a defender, which will allow a wide receiver to properly execute his pass route.

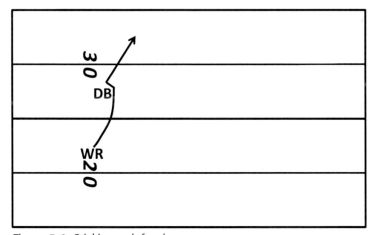

Figure 5-9. Sticking a defender

6

Individual Pass Route Patterns Techniques

Running proper pass route patterns is an art that takes many years to perfect. First, a wide receiver should understand the basic fundamentals and techniques of route running: how to properly release off the line of scrimmage, how to quickly move in and out of his breakpoint, and how to exploit the defensive coverage that's being played against him. Once a wide receiver properly understands the basic fundamentals of pass route running, he then can move on to learning how to master reach individual pass route. This chapter will teach a wide receiver how to efficiently and effectively run the basic individual pass routes commonly used throughout the game of football. Each team and coach might have different parameters for depth and/or the number of steps taken by a wide receiver on each individual pass route, but this chapter uses precise route depths and/or steps taken to best facilitate the teaching process.

Each pass route in a pass pattern should have a purpose and a plan for how a wide receiver is supposed to effectively execute the route. The purpose of the pass route should be clear to a wide receiver for him to run the route successfully. The purpose should be conveyed to a wide receiver during practice and in position meetings. If a wide receiver understands why he's supposed to run a certain pass route when a play is called, he'll better understand how he can execute his assignment. Once the purpose of the pass route is made clear, then a wide receiver should learn how to use the techniques and fundamentals of pass route running and apply them to his individual pass route. This is called *formulating a pass route plan*. Before each play, a wide receiver should have a plan in his mind about how he's going to execute his individual pass route on the upcoming play.

Teaching Progression

Coaches should have a logical order of how they teach pass routes to their wide receivers. A coach can't expect a wide receiver to run a complex pass route like a read route before he learns how to run a hitch route. A wide receiver should master five essential building block pass routes before he can move on to more complex pass routes: the streak, post, hitch, slant, and out pass routes. These five pass routes should be taught and mastered by a wide receiver early on in his career. Each building block route holds techniques and fundamentals that will help a wide receiver master his craft. Elements of the building block routes can be combined together to form a more complex pass route. Once a wide receiver has mastered the building block routes, he'll be ready to contribute effectively in the passing game. A wide receiver can only master the building block routes if his coach has a logical progression for teaching pass route patterns.

Streak Route

The very first time a child plays the game of football, he learns how to "go deep." "Going deep" is another way of saying "run a streak route." Running a streak route is the first pass route a player should master if he's going to become a great wide receiver. The streak route is the building block from which all other pass routes are built. The streak route is the most basic and rudimentary pass route in all of football but can be one of the most difficult routes to master (Figure 6-1).

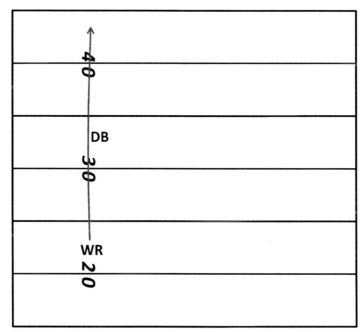

Figure 6-1. Streak route

The idea of a streak route is to stretch a defense vertically down the field. To accomplish this task, a wide receiver should explode out of his stance and break down a defender's cushion as quickly as possible. If a defender is playing off coverage, a wide receiver should break down a defender's cushion and work to "stack" him as quickly as possible. To stack a defender, a wide receiver should beat the defender vertically down the field, then work to position his body directly in front or on top of the defender (Figure 6-2). The key to stacking a defender is for a wide receiver to position his near hip in front of the defender's hip. Once the defender has been stacked, a wide receiver next should work to "hold space."

When running a streak route, a wide receiver should always remember to hold space. Holding space is a concept that requires a wide receiver to push back into a defender's leverage to leave himself enough space along the sideline for the quarterback to deliver the football without having to make a perfect throw. For a coach to effectively teach a wide receiver to hold space, he should use the concept of purgatory. From the bottom of the yard numbers on the field to the sideline is approximately three yards. Purgatory is half of that area (i.e., from the sideline halfway to the bottom of the yard numbers). When running a streak route, a wide receiver doesn't want to run his route into purgatory. Instead, a wide receiver should press into the defender's outside leverage, holding space and not allowing the defender to push him into purgatory

Figure 6-2. The concept of stacking a defender

(Figure 6-3). When a wide receiver doesn't properly hold space and gets pushed into purgatory, he makes it extremely difficult on the quarterback to complete a pass because the throwing window has narrowed (Figure 6-4). The quarterback has more room for error with his pass if a wide receiver can properly hold space against a defender and stay out of purgatory.

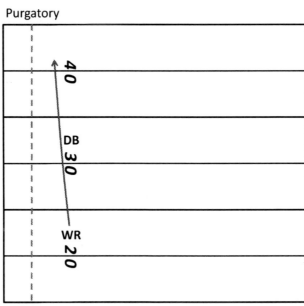

Figure 6-3. Properly holding space away from purgatory

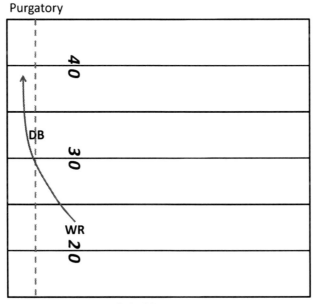

Figure 6-4. Improperly holding space

Once a wide receiver has worked to stack the defender covering him and is properly holding space away from purgatory, he can now worry about properly catching the football. When a running a streak route, a wide receiver should work to catch the football at its highest point, which, as mentioned in Chapter 2, is called *high pointing*. Catching the football at its highest point makes it difficult for a defensive back to shoot his hands through the football and break up a pass. If a wide receiver lets the ball fall below his eye level on a streak throw, it's drastically more likely that a defender will be able to make a play on the football and break up the pass. Being able to high-point the football is the final step a wide receiver needs to take to run an effective streak route.

Post Route

After a wide receiver learns how to run an effective streak route, the next route he can now learn to run is the post route. The post route gets its name from the aim point out of the break that coaches used when first explaining how to run a post route. Coaches would tell a wide receiver to aim for the near goal post, and that's how the post route got its name. For a wide receiver to run an effective post route, he should take away the leverage of the defender who's covering him, step on the defender's toes, stick his route at the breakpoint, and stay thin. If a wide receiver can accomplish these four tasks, he can run an effective post route (Figure 6-5).

Understanding how to take away a defender's leverage is the first key to running the post route. At the snap of the football, a wide receiver should work to get 50/50 leverage on the defender he's running his route off against. Obtaining 50/50 leverage

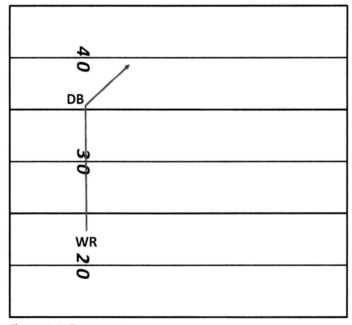

Figure 6-5. Post route

will allow a wide receiver to either break his route inside or outside a defender, which will keep the defender off balance. When running a post route, a wide receiver needs to break his route inside the defender who's covering him. If the defender is aligned inside a wide receiver, he should use a weave stem to work to the defender's inside shoulder to gain 50/50 leverage. If the defender is aligned outside a wide receiver, then a leverage stem can be used to maintain 50/50 leverage. Once a wide receiver has achieved proper leverage, he'll now be in a position to step on the defender's toes and stick the defender at his breakpoint.

After gaining 50/50 leverage, a wide receiver should work to break his route off as close to the defender as possible, which is called *stepping on his toes*. Stepping on his toes will reduce the distance between a wide receiver's breakpoint and the defender, making it difficult for the defender to turn out of his backpedal and run to the direction in which a wide receiver is running his post route.

Once a wide receiver is in a position to step on the defender's toes, he should now stick the defender out of his breakpoint. Sticking a defender requires a wide receiver to combine a hard plant off his outside foot with a slight head fake to the outside away from the direction in which he's breaking his route off (Figure 6-6).

Figure 6-6. Sticking a defender

A wide receiver's goal when running a post route should be to deposit a defender at his break away from the direction he's running his route. This goal can be accomplished with a hard stick plant off his outside foot. Once a wide receiver has successfully deposited the defender with a hard stick plant, all he has to do to win his post route is stay thin away from any oncoming defenders. Staying thin allows a wide receiver the opportunity to catch the football without a potential collision with a defending working into his area. The combination of stepping on the defender's toes, a hard stick, and staying thin will give a wide receiver all the tools necessary to successfully win his post route.

Hitch

The hitch route should be the first intermediate pass route taught by coaches. The fundamentals of the hitch route are incorporated throughout many different pass routes, which makes it essential for coaches to properly teach the different aspects of the route to wide receivers before moving on to more complex pass routes. For a wide receiver to properly run a hitch route, he should sell the route vertically down the field, keep his shoulders down at the breakpoint, and get square to the line of scrimmage (Figure 6-7).

As a wide receiver prepares to run his hitch route, he should remember to burst off the line of scrimmage and sell the idea that he's running a streak route to the defender. This process is called *selling a route vertical*. Every defensive back's biggest fear is getting beat vertically down the field. A wide receiver selling his route vertically

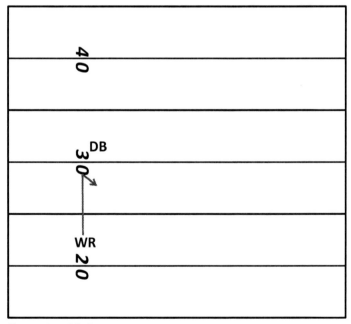

Figure 6-7. Hitch route

will cause the defender to backpedal faster to maintain his cushion against the wide receiver. The maintaining of the cushion by the defender will allow a wide receiver enough space to run his hitch route, which will give the quarterback enough space to throw the hitch route.

Once a wide receiver has sold his route vertically, he can now concentrate on keeping his shoulders down throughout his break and work to get his body square to the line of scrimmage. As a wide receiver enters into the breakpoint phase of his hitch route, he shouldn't let his shoulders rise up. Instead, he needs to keep his shoulders down over his knees, sink his hips, and execute a 180-degree cut (Figure 6-8).

Figure 6-8. Proper shoulder and hip position for a 180-degree cut

If a wide receiver lets his shoulder rise up out of his breakpoint, he'll be making the defender aware that he's breaking off his route. The rising action will cause the defender to start breaking toward the wide receiver, which will potentially give the defender a chance to break up the intended pass. As a wide receiver makes his 180-degree cut, he should make sure his body gets square to the line of scrimmage out of his break. A wide receiver getting his body parallel to the line of scrimmage will allow a quarterback to throw the football to the farthest shoulder away from the defender, which is either a wide receiver's inside or outside shoulder. Whatever shoulder the ball is thrown to is a signal to the wide receiver that he should run after catching the football (Figure 6-9).

If a wide receiver doesn't get his body square to the line of scrimmage, a quarterback's only option is to throw at a wide receiver's inside shoulder. Getting his body square—combined with proper shoulder and hip mechanics for a 180-degree cut—is essential for a wide receiver to execute a proper hitch route.

Figure 6-9. Getting shoulders square to the line of scrimmage

Slant

Like the hitch route, the slant route is one of the basic pass routes a wide receiver should master before he's ready to run more complex pass routes. Teams will utilize multiple different versions of the slant route. Some teams will run their slant routes based on the number of steps a wide receiver will take off the line of scrimmage. Other teams will have a wide receiver work to a certain depth, then break off his route. For example, teams will have a wide receiver explode to five yards, then break off his route. This chapter will explain a three-step slant route. If ran properly, the three-step slant route should take a wide receiver to a depth of five yards from the line of scrimmage before he breaks off his route. For purposes of teaching, this section will explain the three-step slant route versus off coverage first, then move to the slant route versus a pressed defender.

The slant route is a staple for teams that utilize a three-step quick passing game but is often coached incorrectly. The slant route shares a lot of similarities with the post route, but the two should be coached as individual routes. A common mistake in coaching the slant route is lumping it together with the post route and teaching it to a group of wide receivers at the same time. If the two routes are taught together, coaches can minimize the effectiveness of both pass routes and their team's passing game will suffer as a result. To run a proper three-step slant route, a wide receiver should gain inside leverage on a defender, stick his pass route, and take a flat angle out of his breakpoint. Once a wide receiver learns how to accomplish these three coaching points, he'll be able to run an effective three-step slant route versus off coverage (Figure 6-10).

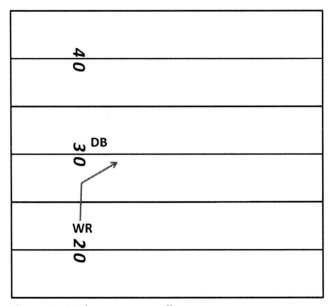

Figure 6-10. Slant route vs. off coverage

Like the post route, the first thing a wide receiver should accomplish when running a three-step slant route is to gain inside leverage on the defender. Proper leverage should be gained on a wide receiver's first step out of his stance. The three-step slant route happens so fast that a wide receiver can't afford to take one false step out of his stance and hope to still maintain the proper inside leverage. If inside leverage isn't achieved, the defender covering a wide receiver will have a free lane to the football and a chance to intercept the pass (Figure 6-11). With inside leverage, a wide receiver puts his entire body between the defender and the football, which makes it difficult for a defender to intercept and break up the pass (Figure 6-12).

Figure 6-11. Improper leverage on the slant route

Figure 6-12. Proper leverage on the slant route

Once a wide receiver has achieved inside leverage, he should then work to stick the defender on the third step of his pass route. When attempting to stick a defender while running a slant route, a wide receiver uses the same technique explained earlier during the post route section of this chapter. A proper stick technique will lead a wide receiver into the breakpoint angle of his slant route. For a wide receiver to properly run a three-step slant route, he should break flat out of his stick plant at a 70-degree angle (Figure 6-13).

Breaking the three-step slant route at the proper angle is the main difference between the post route and the slant route. This is also where coaches tend to make a mistake when teaching the slant route. If the angle of the slant route at the breakpoint is angled too far upfield, a wide receiver will bring himself closer to a defender trying to cover him. Breaking flat will ensure enough room between a wide receiver and the defender to successfully complete the pass. A flat angle at the breakpoint—accompanied with a proper stick on his third step and inside leverage on a defender—will cause a wide receiver to successfully run a three-step slant versus off coverage.

Slant vs. Press

When running a slant route versus press coverage (Figure 6-14), a wide receiver should be very physical at the line of scrimmage. The three-step slant route is a quick-

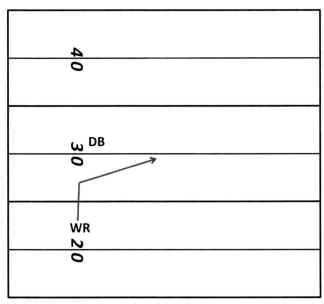

Figure 6-13. Proper angle of the slant route

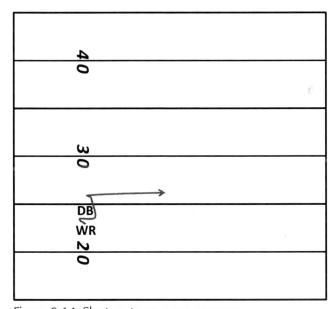

Figure 6-14. Slant route vs. press coverage

hitting pass route, which makes it very important for a wide receiver to win at the line of scrimmage versus press coverage. To effectively run his slant route versus press coverage, a wide receiver should obtain an inside release versus the defender. To obtain an inside release, a wide receiver can use multiple different releases. He can use the widen and slip release, the in-out-in, or the push-off release. All these different releases were mentioned in Chapter 4. No matter what release a wide receiver decides to use, the key is to use a variety of different releases to obtain an inside release. By varying his releases, a wide receiver will keep the pressed defender guessing about what pass route he's trying to run. Once a wide receiver has obtained an inside release, he should work his pass route back into the defender's leverage by pushing his route vertically upfield. Pushing vertical will give the defender the illusion that a wide receiver is running a vertical route, which will cause the defender to start to open up his hips. Once a wide receiver has pushed the defender vertically, he then wants to snap his route off flat and break at a 90-degree angle, as if he were running a dig route. If a wide receiver can be physical at the line of scrimmage, obtain an inside release, push vertically, and snap his route off flat, he'll be able to run a three-step slant route versus press coverage.

Out

The last building block pass route a wide receiver should learn is the out route. The out route incorporates many of the concepts that have already been covered in this chapter, such as selling a pass route vertically and obtaining proper leverage. Also, the out route teaches a wide receiver how to make a 90-degree cut out of his breakpoint, which is an essential skill a wide receiver should incorporate into many other pass routes, such as the dig route. For a wide receiver to properly run an out route, he should sell the route vertically upfield, obtain outside leverage on the defender, and break at a 90-degree angle out of his breakpoint (Figure 6-15).

Like in the hitch and slant routes, a wide receiver should initially sell the idea he's running a streak route to the defender, which is called *selling a route vertically*. Selling his route vertically will help give a wide receiver room to break off his pass route and will make the defender covering him have to honor the vertical threat and potentially

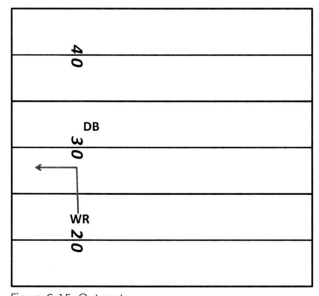

Figure 6-15. Out route

open up his hips to run with the vertical threat. As a wide receiver sells his out route vertically, he should work to obtain outside leverage on the defender covering him. To obtain outside leverage, a wide receiver should use the weave stem technique off the line of scrimmage to properly obtain outside leverage if the defender is already aligned outside of him (Figure 6-16). If the defender is aligned inside of a wide receiver, he should stem at the defender by using the leverage stem technique to maintain outside leverage. The act of stemming at a defender is called *attacking a defender's technique* (Figure 6-17).

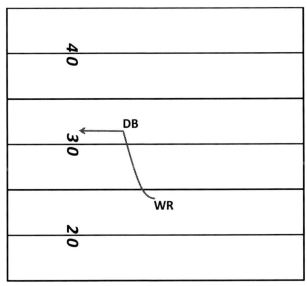

Figure 6-16. Weave stem for an out route

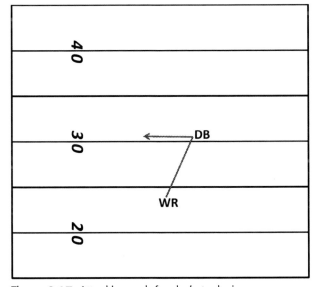

Figure 6-17. Attacking a defender's technique

By attacking a defender off the line of scrimmage, a wide receiver will cause the defender to have to honor the potential threat of an inward-breaking pass route, such as a slant route. The threat of the inward-breaking route will cause the defender to disregard the out route and will give a wide receiver separation from the defender at the breakpoint.

Once outside leverage has been obtained, a wide receiver should finally make sure to break flat at a 90-degree angle out of his breakpoint. If a wide receiver doesn't break flat out of his breakpoint and rounds his cut, it will cause him to drift upfield. The drifting action will give a defender room to undercut the throw from the quarterback and intercept or break up the incoming pass. By breaking flat at a 90-degree angle, a wide receiver eliminates the potential undercut by the defender. Breaking flat at his breakpoint—accompanied with proper outside leverage and the potential vertical threat off the line of scrimmage—will cause a wide receiver to run a fundamentally sound out route.

Second-Level Routes

Once a wide receiver has mastered the building block pass routes, he's then ready to run second-level pass routes. The second-level pass routes use the fundamentals and techniques taught through the building block routes to run more complex pass routes. Each route has elements of a building block route built into it and can only be taught after a wide receiver masters the building block pass routes.

Curl

The curl pass route is basically just a hitch route that's run at a depth that exceeds 10 yards (Figure 6-18). As a wide receiver explodes off the ball, he needs to sell the route vertically to the defender covering him. When running a deeper pass route, such as the Curl, a wide receiver should sell the route vertically. A wide receiver should remember to run full speed through the prescribed depth of his pass route and keep his shoulders on a level plane. If a wide receiver starts to raise his shoulders up and slow down his speed, the defender trying to cover him will be tipped off to the type of route he's running and will start to break toward him to break up the pass. As a wide receiver sells his route vertically, he should work to gain inside leverage on the defender covering him by using a weave stem to properly position himself between the defender and the quarterback. Upon reaching the proper depth of his curl route with inside leverage, a wide receiver should make a 180-degree cut to the inside. As a wide receiver comes out of his breakpoint, he should work back toward the quarterback and attack the football. The football should travel farther down the field when a wide receiver runs a curl route, which makes it very important for a wide receiver to work back to the quarterback out of his breakpoint. If a wide receiver has inside leverage on the defender, works back to the quarterback out of his breakpoint, and attacks the football, he'll have the ability to run a successful curl route.

Comeback

The comeback route requires a wide receiver to use many of the same techniques and fundamentals that are used to run hitch and streak routes. The comeback route is a great complement route for teams that throw a lot of streak routes. The depth of the comeback route varies by coach and preference but is usually run between 14 and 20 yards down the field (Figure 6-19).

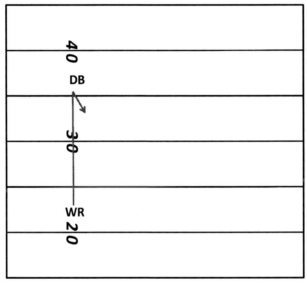

Figure 6-18. Curl route

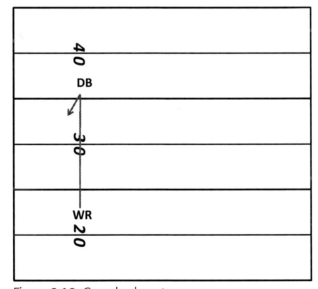

Figure 6-19. Comeback route

If a wide receiver is going to run a successful comeback route, he should sell the route vertically, work to hold space, and cut back down his stem to the football. To successfully run a comeback route, a wide receiver should first sell the idea he's running a streak route to the defender. From the line of scrimmage to the breakpoint, a wide receiver runs the comeback just like he's running a streak route. The idea he's running a streak route will cause the defender to open his hips out of his backpedal. This process takes time, which is why a comeback route is run at depths that exceed 14 yards. As a wide receiver is selling his route vertically, he needs to remember to work into a defender's outside leverage to hold space away from the sideline. By properly holding space, a wide receiver will give himself enough room to the outside to run his comeback route. Once a wide receiver has reached his breakpoint, he should make a 180-degree cut to the outside toward the sideline and work to get his shoulders square to the line of scrimmage, like in a hitch route. Like in a curl route, a wide receiver should attack the football out of his breakpoint. If he doesn't attack the football, a wide receiver will give the defender a chance to break up the pass. A wide receiver should expect the football to be thrown to his outside shoulder. At this point, if a wide receiver has sold the route vertically, given himself enough space, and attacks the football out of his breakpoint, he should be able to easily run a successful comeback route.

Dig

The dig route is an inward-breaking route that's run at a depth between 10 and 20 yards. The depth of the dig route varies by team and what type of passing scheme it's running. Whether a dig route is run at 12 or 20 yards, the technique that's required to properly run the route stays the same. The dig route combines the approach phase of a post route with the breakpoint mechanics of an out route (Figure 6-20).

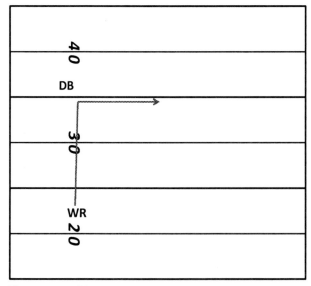

Figure 6-20. Dig route

To properly run a dig route, a wide receiver should sell the route vertically, gain inside leverage on the defender who's covering him, and break flat out of his breakpoint. Like all the pass routes mentioned in this chapter, the first step to running a proper dig route is to sell the route vertical. For the dig route, a wide receiver wants to sell the idea to the defender that he's running a post route. As a wide receiver enters into the approach phase of his route, he wants to sell the dig route vertically and make the defender open his hips to turn and run out of his backpedal. The approach phase of the dig route is the exact same as the post route up until the breakpoint. Like in the post route, a wide receiver wants to gain inside leverage on the defender who's trying to cover him. If the defender is aligned inside of him, a wide receiver can use a weave stem to take inside leverage from the defender. If he's aligned outside a wide receiver, he can use a leverage stem to maintain inside leverage.

Gaining proper leverage—combined with selling the dig route vertically—will help a wide receiver come open upon reaching his breakpoint. As a wide receiver reaches his breakpoint, he should sink his hips and keep his shoulders down over his knees and toes. Proper breakpoint fundamentals will allow a wide receiver to make a crisp 90-degree cut and come out of his breakpoint flat without drifting upfield. For most dig routes, a wide receiver should come out of his breakpoint flat and stay on the move. A wide receiver never wants to drift upfield out of his breakpoint when running a dig route. Drifting upfield will give the defender covering a wide receiver room to undercut the throw and possibly intercept the pass. If a wide receiver can sell the route vertical, gain inside leverage, and come out of his break flat, he'll be able to properly run a dig route for his team.

Corner

A corner route requires a wide receiver to use the same techniques and fundamentals as he would if he were running a post route. The difference between the two routes occurs at the breakpoint. A corner route is an outward-breaking route that's mainly run by an inside slot receiver, whereas a post route is an inward-breaking route. The fundamentals of a corner route are very similar to a post route. When running a corner route, a wide receiver wants to sell the route vertically, step on a defender's toes, and stick the defender out of his break. These fundamentals—combined with setting a high angle out of his break—will allow a wide receiver to run a proper corner route (Figure 6-21).

As a wide receiver enters into the approach phase of his pass route, he wants to work to get 50/50 leverage on the defender covering him. This 50/50 leverage will make it difficult for the defender to decide if a wide receiver is running an inward-breaking route or an outward-breaking route. Like in the post route, once 50/50 leverage has been achieved, a wide receiver wants to make sure he steps on the defender's toes as he makes his stick plant. Sticking the defender is crucial to running an effective corner route. The stick plant will help ensure a wide receiver comes out of

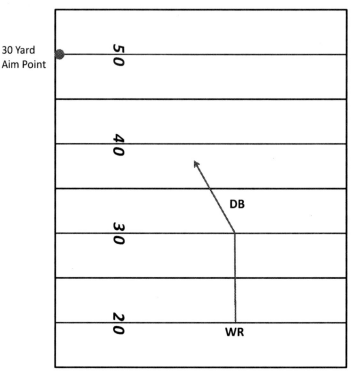

Figure 6-21. Corner route

his breakpoint at a sharp, crisp angle. Another option a wide receiver has when running a corner route instead of a stick plant is to use a three-step move. A three-step move requires a wide receiver to first make an outside plant toward the direction he's running his corner route. His second step is then back inside, like he's running a post route. His third and final step in his breakpoint is then back toward his corner route (Figure 6-22). The three-step move will cause the defender to freeze in his backpedal because he doesn't know which way a wide receiver to truly trying to break. The three-step move can be a very effective technique for a wide receiver when running a corner route.

Once a wide receiver has made either a crisp stick plant or a three-step move, he should then set a high angle. Out of his breakpoint, a wide receiver wants to set his angle of departure 30 yards down the field from where his initial alignment was (Figure 6-22). The 30-yard angle will give the quarterback a clean throwing window to deliver the football. By having a high angle, the quarterback has the opportunity to read the defense and either drop a throw over the top of the defense or throw a flat pass to lead the wide receiver away from the defender trying to cover him. If a wide receiver's angle is too shallow, the quarterback's options for how he can deliver the pass become very limited. If a wide receiver can incorporate a high angle with a crisp breakpoint and the proper leverage, he'll be able to run an effective corner route.

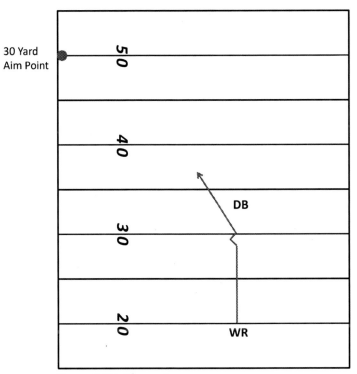

Figure 6-22. Three-step corner move

7

Wide Receiver Blocking

Every wide receiver wants to run pass routes, catch passes, and score touchdowns, but for a wide receiver to truly become a great football player, he should be able to block downfield. Downfield blocking at the wide receiver position is all about attitude and effort. Any wide receiver can become a great downfield blocker if he can develop an aggressive attitude and is willing to exert effort. Four- and five-yard runs are created at the point of attack by the offensive line, but 10- and 15-yard runs are created by wide receiver blocking. Having wide receivers who are great run blockers adds an extra dimension to any offense. If an offense's wide receivers can block, the likelihood of a run play turning into a long touchdown run will increase.

Aggressive Downfield Blocking Attitude and Effort

For a wide receiver to become a great downfield blocker, he should develop an aggressive attitude and learn to give 100 percent effort on every play. Developing an aggressive attitude starts with the wide receivers coach. The wide receivers coach should make run blocking an important part of the weekly practice schedule. If run blocking fundamentals are neglected, then the wide receivers coach can't expect his players to display the proper attitude or effort when it comes to run blocking. The wide receivers coach should teach his players how to be aggressive with their downfield blocking techniques. He should make run blocking drills aggressive, physical, and competitive. Players should be rewarded for how many pancake blocks and cut blocks they achieve during a game. Also, plays where a wide receiver shows great effort and an aggressive attitude should be rewarded. The wide receivers coach should keep year-long stats on how many pancake blocks, cut blocks, and effort blocks a player makes. Keeping these stats and rewarding the leaders will keep a wide receiver involved in the run game.

To play with an aggressive attitude and with 100 percent effort on the game field, a wide receiver should learn to do so on the practice field. Making blocking drills during practice physical, aggressive, and competitive will help teach wide receivers how to be aggressive and play with great effort. Run blocking drills during practice shouldn't be the time to slow the tempo of practice down; instead, run blocking drills should be used to make practice more competitive and aggressive. A wide receiver will never become a great downfield blocker if run blocking drills are slowed down and are less physical than other drills. If a coach wants a wide receiver to become a great downfield blocker, he should develop the wide receiver's aggressive attitude in practice, which will cause the receiver to play with great effort on game day and be a force for the offense in the run game.

Stalk Blocking

The most common kind of block used in football by a wide receiver is the stalk block. The key to the stalk block is for a wide receiver to be aggressive coming off the line of scrimmage, selling a vertical streak pass route for at least three yards. A wide receiver should attack a defender with his initial start off the line of scrimmage, selling a streak pass route. After selling a streak pass route, a wide receiver should be able to break down early enough in front of a defender to catch his movement. *Catching a defender's movement* is the term used to describe how a wide receiver positions himself once a defender recognizes that it's a run play. Catching a defender's movement in the open field is one of the hardest things in football to accomplish. A wide receiver should break down early in front of a defender and anticipate which direction a defender is going to break at the football; once the defender breaks, a wide receiver should move his feet to get between the defender and the football. If a wide receiver can successfully catch a defender's movement, then he'll be in a great position to execute a stalk block (Figure 7-1).

Stalk Blocking Eye Placement Fundamentals

For a wide receiver to properly execute a stalk block in the open field, he should know how to properly position his eyes. As a wide receiver releases off the line of scrimmage, his eyes should be fixed on his target, who's the defender he's assigned to block. A wide receiver's eyes need to be up throughout the whole play. His aim point should be the defender's numbers. If a wide receiver fixes his aim point too low on a defender's body, his head will be more likely to drop as he attempts a stalk block. A wide receiver doesn't want to fix his eyes on the defender's eyes or head. Having a high aim point

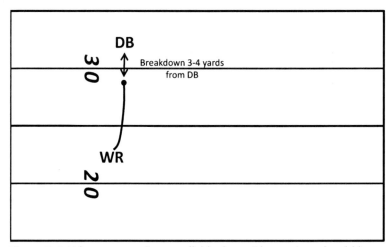

Figure 7-1. When attempting a stalk block, a wide receiver should burst off the line of scrimmage, selling a vertical streak pass route. Then, he should break down at least three yards in front of a defender and prepare to catch a defender's movement.

will make it easier for a defender to use his eyes and head to fake out a wide receiver. If a wide receiver properly positions his eyes on a defender's numbers, then he'll have perfect eye positioning to catch a defender's movement while still ensuring his head will be up throughout his stalk block. Proper eye placement will also help a wide receiver play with the proper pad level. Positioning his eyes on a defender's numbers will help a wide receiver maintain a low pad level throughout his stalk block. A wide receiver should maintain a pad level lower than the defender's if he wants to properly execute a stalk block.

Stalk Blocking Hand and Arm Position Fundamentals

When a wide receiver attempts a stalk block, he should understand how to properly position his hands and arms. Once a wide receiver is at the point in his stalk block where he needs to make contact with a defender, he should use his hands and arms to deliver the initial blow to a defender. Right before the initial blow, a wide receiver should cock his arms back and be ready to shoot forward aggressively. When delivering his initial strike, a wide receiver should aggressively and violently shoot his arms at the defender's chest. The arms and elbows should be close to the body, and his aim point should be for the hands to strike a defender right above a wide receiver's eye level. When a wide receiver's hands strike the defender, the wide receiver's thumbs should be up and the palms should be positioned out. Proper hand position will ensure that a wide receiver's elbow stay close to the body and don't bow out. A wide receiver wants to keep his hands within the framework of a defender's shoulder pads. If a wide receiver's hands strike outside the framework of a defender's shoulder pads, he more than likely will be called for a holding penalty. Once a wide receiver has delivered his initial blow with proper arm and hand fundamentals, he should work to lock his arms out and should then finish his block with his feet. If a defender attempts to push into a wide receiver, he should continue to work to lock out the arms and keep his feet moving. If a defender steps back, a wide receiver should recoil his arms and hands and prepare to catch the defender's movement again and reshoot his arms and hands.

Stalk Blocking Foot Position Fundamentals

Accompanied with proper eye, hand, and arm placement, a wide receiver should also understand how to use his feet to properly position himself to execute a perfect stalk block. Once a wide receiver has broken down at least three yards in front of a defender by using his catch movement technique, he should make sure his feet are shoulder-width apart and his weight is evenly distributed on the balls of his feet. His knees need to be bent, and he should have a low center of gravity. From this athletic position, a wide receiver will be in the proper position to catch a defender's movement.

Once a wide receiver has initiated contact with a defender with a proper hand and arm strike, it's time for his feet to finish the stalk block for him. Upon contact with a defender, a wide receiver should fire his feet by using quick, short, choppy steps. These steps are designed to create power and drive a defender back. If a wide receiver doesn't fire his feet on contact with a defender, he won't be able to generate enough power to properly finish his stalk block. Once contact is made and his feet begin to fire, a wide receiver should continue to fire his feet until the stalk block is executed. Throughout his stalk block, a wide receiver should make sure to keep his feet shoulder-width apart. As a defender is driven back, he needs to work his hips and feet upfield with the defender. Many wide receivers make the mistake of firing their feet and hips in one spot instead of moving them upfield. Leaving the hips and feet behind will cause a wide receiver to fall off and lose his leverage and position on a defender.

To successfully execute a stalk block, a wide receiver should have his eyes positioned properly at the defender's numbers; his thumbs need to be up, with his palms out; and his arms need to be tight to the body to deliver a devastating strike to a defender. Upon delivering his initial strike, a wide receiver should fire his feet by using quick, short, choppy steps. His feet should keep firing until the stalk block is finished. If all this is done, a wide receiver will be able to properly execute a stalk block.

Walk-Off Block

The walk-off block is used when a wide receiver needs to come out of his stance already broken down and catch a defender's movement as soon as the football is snapped. A walk-off block is good to use when a wide receiver is blocking for a bubble screen pass or should block a pressed defender or an alley defender who's aligned within five yards of a wide receiver. The walk-off block uses the same basic principles as a stalk block. The difference between the two blocks is the initial get-off at the snap of the football.

When using a walk-off block, a wide receiver will come out of his stance already broken down. Just like in a stalk block, his feet need to be shoulder-width apart and the knees need to be bent, with his weight distributed evenly over the balls of his feet. A wide receiver's eyes need to be instantly fixed on his assigned defender's numbers. He should instantly be ready to move his feet to catch the defender's movement. The key to the walk-off block is if a defender doesn't react right away, then a wide receiver can walk himself closer to the defender's position while still maintaining a low center of gravity and a great athletic position (Figure 7-2). Once contact is made with a defender, a wide receiver should fire his feet aggressively and, like in a stalk block, drive his feet through a defender until his block is finished.

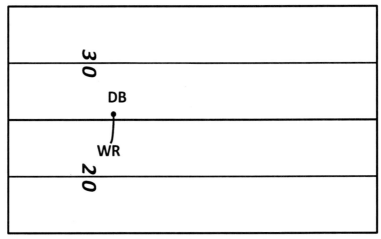

Figure 7-2. Using the walk-off block, a wide receiver should come out of his stance already broken down and should be prepared to catch a defender's movement.

Read Force Block

A read force block is used by a wide receiver when his assignment is to block the run force defender on any given run play. The read force block is especially useful against teams that play a lot of quarters coverage and like to use their safeties as force defenders in the run game. To execute a read force block, a wide receiver should do a great job in his pre-snap scan, recognizing the defense's coverage. At the snap of the football, a wide receiver should first read the safety nearest to him. If the safety steps back, then the wide receiver turns and blocks the cornerback. If the near safety steps forward, then the wide receiver takes a flat angle and goes to block the safety. The key to the read force block is for a wide receiver to take a flat initial angle off the line of scrimmage. A wide receiver shouldn't gain ground with his first step; instead, his first step should be lateral and flat down the line of scrimmage. By taking a flat lateral step, a wide receiver will put himself in the proper position to block a run force safety if he needs to. When blocking a run force safety, a wide receiver should anticipate where the safety is going to end up and not set his aim point where the safety is initially aligned. Anticipating where a run force safety will end up will put a wide receiver in the proper position to execute his read force block (Figure 7-3).

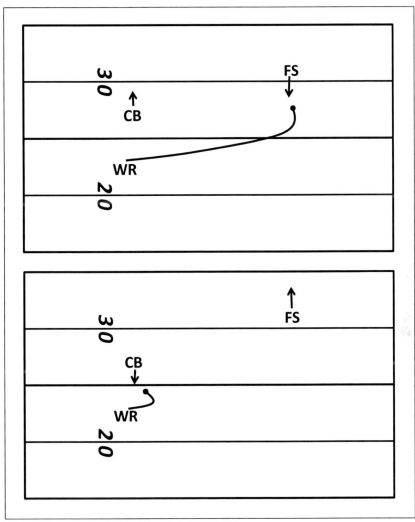

Figure 7-3. Using a read force block, a wide receiver should first read the near safety. If the near safety steps forward, the wide receiver will take a flat angle and anticipate where the safety will end up (top). By taking a flat angle, a wide receiver will help ensure he can properly execute his read force block. If the safety backs up, the wide receiver will turn and block the cornerback (bottom).

Cutoff Block

A cutoff block is when a slot wide receiver should cut off and block a defender who's aligned inside of him. At the snap of the football, a wide receiver should take a flat angle and attempt to cut off an alley defender from making a tackle on the running back. A wide receiver's aim point should be the inside shoulder of the alley defender. Once he reaches his aim point, a wide receiver should square his shoulders to the alley defender, strike him with his thumbs up and palms out, and quickly drive his feet until the block is executed properly. For the cutoff block to be executed properly, a wide receiver should take a flat angle out of his stance. His first step should be lateral down the line of scrimmage, and he should anticipate and aim for where an alley defender is going to be—out where he's aligned pre-snap. To help a wide receiver make a cutoff block, he can flip his stance and put his inside foot back. Putting the inside foot back will help a slot wide receiver execute a cutoff block quicker (Figure 7-4).

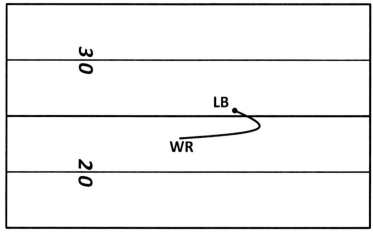

Figure 7-4. Cutoff block technique

Convoy Block

A convoy block is used by a wide receiver when he's on the backside of a run play. The convoy block requires a wide receiver to attempt to block a backside safety who might be in position to tackle a running back if he's broken through the second level of the defense. The convoy block can also be referred to as a touchdown block. To properly execute a convoy block requires a wide receiver to play with effort. The convoy block epitomizes a wide receiver's effort and attitude about run blocking. At the snap of the football, a wide receiver should take a flat angle and sprint as fast as possible to block the backside safety. Going full speed on a convoy block will be the difference as to whether a wide receiver makes a successful block. If a wide receiver is assigned a convoy block, his goal should be to make a touchdown block. His effort to go block the backside safety will determine if he can accomplish his goal. It's easy for many wide receivers to take a play off when assigned a convoy block. Great wide receivers put forth the extra effort needed to properly execute a convoy block (Figure 7-5).

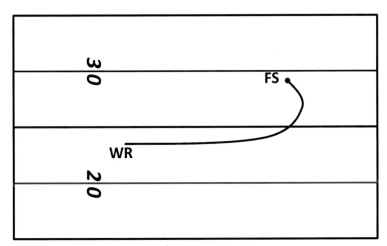

Figure 7-5. Convoy block technique

Crack Block

The crack block is a common block used by a wide receiver to knock an inside defender off his feet. Before the football is snapped, a wide receiver who's assigned a crack block should make sure he's not aligned so wide he can't properly execute a crack block. At the snap of the football, a wide receiver should take a flat angle down the line of scrimmage and aim for where a defender is going to be, not where he's initially aligned. A wide receiver needs to make sure his crack block is above a defender's waist. Upon making contact, a wide receiver should keep his head up and position it in front of the defender's body. The key to executing a crack block is for a wide receiver to be aggressive and physical and to never hesitate. After making contact with a defender, a wide receiver should continue to explode his feet and body through a defender until he's been knocked down. If a wide receiver runs full speed, has his head positioned in front, and explodes his body and feet through a defender, he'll be able to properly execute a crack block (Figure 7-6).

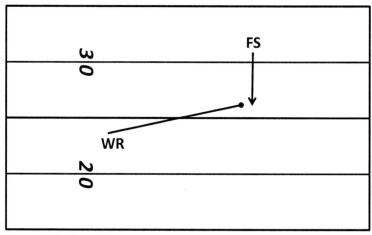

Figure 7-6. Crack block

Cut Block

Another very common block a wide receiver will use is the cut block. The cut block is designed to slow down a defender who's bull-rushing a wide receiver. The cut block is also designed to chop a defender down to the ground. The design of a cut block makes it ideal for a wide receiver to use against aggressive and physical defenders who like to bull-rush a wide receiver when he's attempting to stalk block a defender. A key to a cut block is for a wide receiver to be patient and let a defender close the ground between himself and a wide receiver. When performing a cut block, a wide receiver should try to use a defender's momentum against him to cut the defender down to the ground. If a defender isn't being aggressive and is hanging back, a wide receiver shouldn't attempt to perform a cut block; instead, he should execute a stalk block.

The cut block can be dangerous to a defender's legs and knees. Because of the danger posed by a cut block, very specific rules determine when a wide receiver can cut a defender. For high school wide receivers, the cut block is illegal. For college wide receivers, the cut block can only be used at certain times and places on the football field. A cut block can be used if a wide receiver is aligned inside the tackle box and is cutting a defender who's also aligned inside the tackle box. A cut block can be used if a wide receiver is aligned inside the tackle box and moves outside the tackle box to cut a defender (Figure 7-7). If a wide receiver is aligned outside the tackle box, he can't come inside into the tackle box and cut a defender unless he's positioned himself so his shoulders are parallel with the front of a defender (Figure 7-8). Also, when attempting to cut a defender, a wide receiver can never throw himself into the side of a defender's body or into his back. A cut block can be made only when a wide receiver is positioned squarely in front of a defender and he's cutting the front of a defender's body (Figure 7-9).

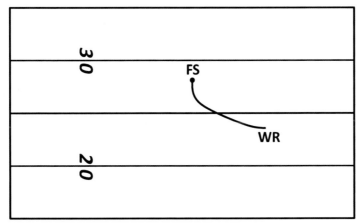

Figure 7-7. Inside the tackle box to outside cut block

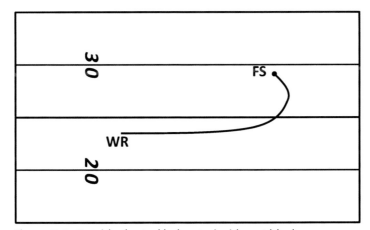

Figure 7-8. Outside the tackle box to inside cut block

Figure 7-9. Proper cut block position

Cut Blocking Head and Eye Placement Fundamentals

When a wide receiver attempts a cut block, he should always keep his head up. If a wide receiver dips his head and eyes, it becomes very easy for a defender to avoid his cut block attempt. Also, if a wide receiver dips his head, he puts his neck in a dangerous position and he could be injured when attempting a cut block. A wide receiver should keep his head up throughout his cut block so he can see his target area. When attempting a cut block, a wide receiver should have a very specific aiming point on a defender's body. When performing a cut block, a wide receiver should fix his eyes on a defender's thigh board. A defender's thigh board is the proper aim point for a wide receiver to execute a cut block (Figure 7-10).

Figure 7-10. Proper aim point for a cut block

Cut Blocking Feet and Hands Fundamentals

When a wide receiver attempts a cut block, he should use proper feet and arm fundamentals to execute his cut block. Like in a stalk block, a wide receiver should fire out of his stance and break down three to four yards in front of his target. Once he's squarely in front of his target, a wide receiver can prepare to perform a cut block. From a good athletic position, a wide receiver should be patient and wait for the perfect moment to cut block a defender. A wide receiver should always step first with the foot opposite in the direction of his leverage when attempting a cut block. For example, when attempting to block the defender's outside shoulder, a wide receiver should step with his inside foot. If a wide receiver needed to block the defender's inside shoulder, he'd step with his outside foot. No matter which foot he steps with, the aim point for a wide receiver's first step is the defender's crouch.

Once a wide receiver has taken his first step at the defender's crouch, he should lower his body and rip his arm opposite his leverage—upward and through the defender's crouch. Like with his feet, if a wide receiver is blocking the defender's outside shoulder, he'll rip his inside foot and arm through the crouch of a defender. If he's aiming at the inside shoulder of a defender, he'll rip his outside foot and arm through the crouch of a defender. After ripping his arm through the defender's crouch, a wide receiver should then drive his shoulder opposite his leverage through the thigh board of a defender. At the same time he drives his shoulder through a defender's thigh board, a wide receiver should keep driving his feet, taking quick, short, choppy steps forward through a defender. If the exploding action of a wide receiver's shoulder and feet through the thigh board of a defender doesn't knock him down, a wide receiver should try to bear-crawl through the defender to keep him occupied and out of range to make a tackle on the ball carrier.

Blocking Drills

Drill #1: Stalk Blocking

The stalk blocking drill is designed to teach a wide receiver the proper techniques and fundamentals of a stalk block (Figure 7-11). All the wide receivers need to be in one line, with one player opposite the line acting as the defender. At the snap of the football, the first wide receiver in line sprints out of his stance and breaks down three to four yards in front of the defender. The defender works into the wide receiver. After making contact with the defender, the wide receiver drives the defender back until the coach blows his whistle to stop play. After the wide receiver works on stalking a defender who's right in front of him, the coach can move the angle to which the defender breaks to simulate a more game-like blocking situation.

Coaching Points

- The wide receiver should have his head up and his eyes focused on the defender's breast plate.
- He should break down three to four yards in front of the defender.
- He should strike the defender with his thumbs up and palms out. The hands need to be positioned tight to the body and within the framework of the defender.
- He should drive his feet through the whistle by using quick, short, choppy steps.
- He should be physical and aggressive.

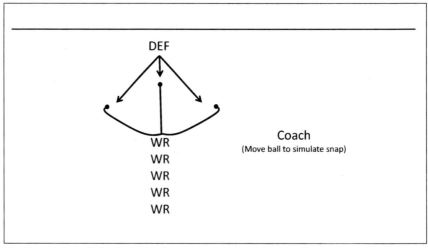

Figure 7-11. Stalk blocking drill

Drill #2: Catching the Defender's Movement

The catch movement drill is designed to teach a wide receiver how to react quickly to a defender's movement (Figure 7-12). Also, the catch movement drill is used to teach a wide receiver proper eye placement fundamentals. At the snap of the football, the first wide receiver in lines bursts at the defender who's positioned 15 yards away. The wide receiver needs to break down three to four yards in front of the defender, then walk his block up to the defender, keeping a low athletic position. During the walkup time, the defender needs to start moving side to side as quickly as possible, trying to fake the wide receiver out. The wide receiver needs to focus his eyes on the defender's breast plate and move his feet in the direction the defender is moving, keeping his body squarely in front of the defender's body. The wide receiver and defender keep moving until the coach has blown his whistle.

Coaching Points

- The wide receiver should have his head up and his eyes focused on the defender's breast plate.
- He should break down three to four yards in front of the defender.
- He should move his feet quickly, keeping his knees bent and his body in an athletic position.
- He should quickly and efficiently react to the defender's movement.

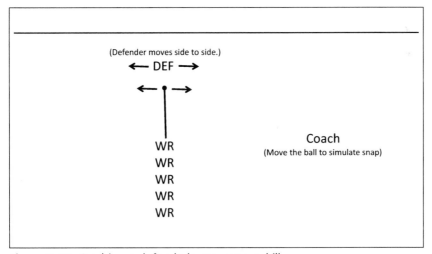

Figure 7-12. Catching a defender's movement drill

Drill #3: Angle Cutoff Blocking

The angle cutoff blocking drill is designed to teach a wide receiver how to properly execute a cutoff block on a defender who's aligned inside of him (Figure 7-13). At the snap of the football, the wide receiver needs to take a flat lateral first step with his inside foot. Taking a flat track to the defender will allow the wide receiver to cut off the defender and get his shoulders square to the defender throughout his block. After completing the drill to one side, the defender should flip to the other side of the wide receiver line so the group can execute a cutoff block to each side.

Coaching Points

- The wide receiver should take a flat lateral first step and anticipate where the defender is going to end up.
- He shouldn't aim where he's aligned pre-snap.
- He should have his head up and his eyes focused on the defender's breast plate.
- He should strike the defender with his thumbs up and palms out. The hands need to be positioned tight to the body and within the framework of the defender.
- He should drive his feet through the whistle by using quick, short, choppy steps.
- He should be physical and aggressive.

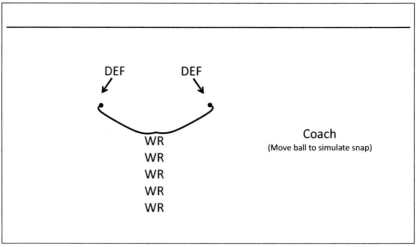

Figure 7-13. Angle cutoff blocking drill

Drill #4: Read Force Blocking

The read force drill is designed to teach a wide receiver how to read coverage so he can correctly identify and block the defense's run force defender (Figure 7-14). At the snap of the football, the first wide receiver up reads the safety aligned inside of him. If the safety moves forward, the wide receiver takes a flat lateral angle and anticipates where the safety is going to end up. If the safety moves backward, the wide receiver turns back and blocks the corner aligned over the top of him. The coach will tell the safety and corner what to do without the wide receiver being able to see.

Coaching Points

- The wide receiver should take a flat lateral first step and anticipate where the defender is going to end up.
- He shouldn't aim where he's aligned pre-snap.
- He should keep his head up and his eyes focused on the safety to find out what the read is.
- He should strike the defender with his thumbs up and palms out. The hands need to be positioned tight to the body and within the framework of the defender.
- He should drive his feet through the whistle by using quick, short, choppy steps.
- He should be physical and aggressive.

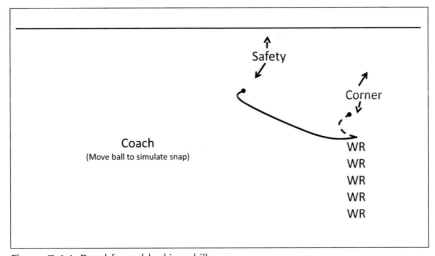

Figure 7-14. Read force blocking drill

Drill #5: Crack Blocking

The crack blocking drill is designed to teach a wide receiver how to properly execute a crack block against a defender (Figure 7-15). The crack block drill is a great drill to make competitive and incorporate the whole defensive back group against the whole wide receiver group because it's also a great drill to teach defenders how to play and replace the crack block. At the snap of the football, the first wide receiver in line takes a flat angle and anticipates where a defender is going to end up. His aim point when he meets the defender should be the defender's ear hole. He'll deliver a crack block to the defender trying to knock him to the ground. At the same time this is happening, a ballcarrier is running a toss play and the defender is trying to make a play on the ball.

Coaching Points

- The wide receiver should take a flat lateral first step and anticipate where the defender is going to end up.
- He shouldn't aim where he's aligned pre-snap.
- He should aim for the defender's ear hole.
- He should drive his feet through the whistle by using quick, short, choppy steps.
- He should be physical and aggressive.

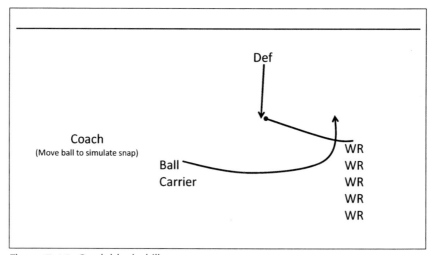

Figure 7-15. Crack block drill

Drill #6: Convoy Blocking (Touchdown Drill)

The convoy blocking drill teaches a wide receiver what kind of attitude and effort it takes to make a convoy block (Figure 7-16). At the snap of the football, the first wide receiver in line needs to take a flat angle and run full speed to make the convoy block at the defender aligned inside of him. The defender should be at least 10 yards inside of the wide receiver and should run three-fourths speed at an angle away from the wide receiver. If a wide receiver doesn't go full speed in this drill, he'll never be able to catch the defender. This drill can also be called the touchdown block drill. Coaches should encourage their wide receivers to be the ones who make the touchdown block.

Coaching Points

- The wide receiver should take a flat lateral first step and anticipate where the defender is going to end up.
- He shouldn't aim where he's aligned pre-snap.
- He should exhibit effort and willingness to execute a convoy block.
- He should make the touchdown block
- He should drive his feet through the whistle by using quick, short, choppy steps.
- He should be physical and aggressive.

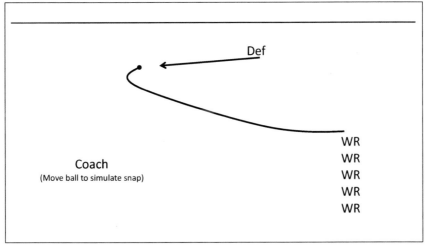

Figure 7-16. Convoy blocking drill

Drill #7: Cut Blocking

The cut block drill is designed to teach a wide receiver how to properly perform a cut block against a defender (Figure 7-17). In this drill, the entire secondary is working against all the wide receivers. The cut blocking drill is designed to be very competitive and physical. At the snap of the football, the wide receiver closes ground between himself and the defensive back. After breaking down, the wide receiver tries to cut block the defender. The defender backpedals at the snap of the football, then breaks forward and tries to make a tackle on the ballcarrier, who's running a bubble screen pass route. This drill allows wide receivers to work on blocking and running with the football.

Coaching Points

- The wide receiver should take a flat lateral first step and anticipate where the defender is going to end up.
- He should break down three to four yards in front of the defender.
- He should aim for the defender's outside shoulder and his eyes should be fixed on the defender's thigh board.
- He should step with his inside foot and rip the inside arm through the defender's crouch.
- He should drive his inside shoulder through the defender's thigh board.
- He should drive his feet through the whistle by using quick, short, choppy steps.
- He should be physical and aggressive.

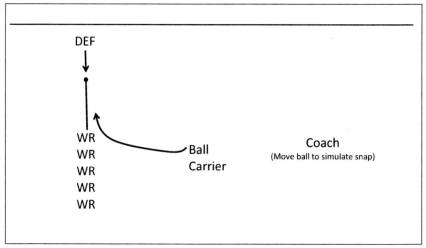

Figure 7-17. Cut blocking drill

Drill #8: Stalk and Cut Blocking

The stalk and cut blocking drill is designed to teach a wide receiver when to decide if a cut block or a stalk block should be used (Figure 7-18). The wide receiver at the snap of the football needs to read the defender. If the defender is bull-rushing him, then he should perform a cut block. If the defender is playing off the wide receiver, then he should execute a stalk block. The defender will try to make a tackle on the ballcarrier after initially backpedaling off the snap of the football. This drill is supposed to be very competitive and physical. The entire secondary and wide receivers need to be involved in this drill.

Coaching Points

- The wide receiver should have his head up and his eyes focused on the defender's breast plate.
- He should break down three to four yards in front of the defender.
- He should read the defender's movement to decide if a stalk block or a cut block is necessary.
- He should execute great stalk or cut blocking techniques and fundamentals.
- He should drive his feet through the whistle by using quick, short, choppy steps.
- He should be physical and aggressive.
- He should compete with great attitude and effort.

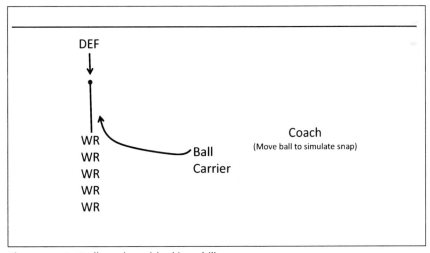

Figure 7-18. Stalk and cut blocking drill

8

Recognizing Pass Coverage

Teams today run complex passing schemes that adjust on the fly to beat all sorts of different coverages. For teams to be able to run these complex passing schemes, the wide receivers group must be able to recognize coverages and adjust their pass routes to beat the coverage being played. For a wide receiver to become a complete player, he should be able to understand an opponent's defense and recognize pass coverage. A wide receiver can be the most physically gifted player on the field with great speed, hands, and jumping ability, but if he can't recognize the coverage a defense is playing, he'll never reach his full potential. Off the field, a wide receiver should put in extra time watching game film of an opponent to understand their tendencies. On the field, a wide receiver should have great vision, take advantage of his pre-snap scan, and see the moving picture after the football is snapped. When a wide receiver can combine the information he's gained from studying film with great field vision, he'll be able to recognize an opponent's coverage on a regular basis.

Off-the-Field Preparation

At all times throughout the year, a wide receiver can always watch film of a future opponent or a certain scheme or skill he's looking to improve. Watching film will help a wide receiver understand what scheme the upcoming opponent runs. Also, it will help a wide receiver have a better idea of the strengths and weaknesses of the opponent and its scheme. For a wide receiver to get the most out of each film session, his coach should provide him with proper guidelines for watching opponent film. Some general guidelines a coach could give his wide receivers group include:

- What plays are we running out of the formation shown? What would you anticipate happening if particular plays were called from a certain formation? Walk through a play call in your mind.
- What's the coverage? What are tips that will help me identify the coverage during the game? Look at your coverage triangle. Examples: depth of safeties, linebacker alignment, eyes of linebackers and corners.
- What's the situation in the game? You need to know down and distance on every play; third down will play a lot different from first down. Is the situation late in the game? What coverage do they play in a two-minute situation? What do they do when you're in the red zone?
- You should know the number each position wears so you can recognize the way the defense aligns, so you can determine if they're in a different personnel group (nickel), and so you can tell if they have differences in the coverages they play when they change personnel. Have a depth chart with you when watching film.
- If pressure or a blitz occurs, what are the indicators? Safety rotation, linebacker tilt, one technique. Are they a field or boundary pressure team? What's their favorite blitz down? Also, know what coverage the opponent plays when bringing certain pressures.
- Think about the different pass route concepts we'll run versus each type of pressure. Do we need to sight adjust versus the given pressure? Do they like to blitz one safety or linebacker more than another?
- Who's the better run support player? Who's the best cover linebacker, safety and corner?
- Try to catch yourself when you're daydreaming or not paying attention to the details of the film. Keep in mind that when you sit down to watch the film that you'll truly benefit by becoming more comfortable with your opponent. Nothing feels worse than sitting in the locker room after a game and knowing you could have prepared more.

Having proper guidelines for watching film will ensure that a wide receiver knows what to look for, and they'll help in his game preparation. If a coach doesn't have guidelines, his wide receivers group won't be as prepared as they potentially could be for each game.

Pre-Snap Scan

From the moment the huddle breaks to the time the ball is snapped, a wide receiver should keep his eyes fixed on the opponent's secondary to identify what coverage the defense is going to play. The process a wide receiver performs before the snap of every play is called the pre-snap scan. Using proper pre-snap scan fundamentals varies by what position on the field a wide receiver is playing. If a wide receiver is aligning as an outside receiver, he'll perform a different pre-snap scan from when he's aligning as a slot receiver. Regardless of what position a wide receiver is playing, the pre-snap scan will give him the necessary information to be able to identify an opponent's coverage at the snap of the football.

Outside Receiver Pre-Snap Scan

Before every snap of the football, an outside receiver needs to use his eyes to scan the field and perform a pre-snap scan. The pre-snap scan should be used by an outside receiver to identify his coverage triangle (Figure 8-1).

The first thing an outside receiver should do is identify the safeties on the field. Using the information from his scouting report, a wide receiver should know what numbers the safeties wear, which will help him identify who the safeties are and determine their location on the field. After identifying the safeties' locations, a wide receiver should analyze their postures and positioning to help determine what coverage they're going to play. The positioning of the nearest safety to a wide receiver's alignment will be the safety included in an outside receiver's coverage triangle. (Tips for identifying specific coverages are covered later in this chapter.)

Once the safeties are identified, an outside receiver needs to indentify the cornerback over the top of him, which is the next step for a wide receiver to identify his coverage triangle. Like with the safeties, a wide receiver should know what number the cornerbacks wear and analyze their postures and positioning to identify coverage. The final step to an outside receiver's pre-snap scan and coverage triangle is find the

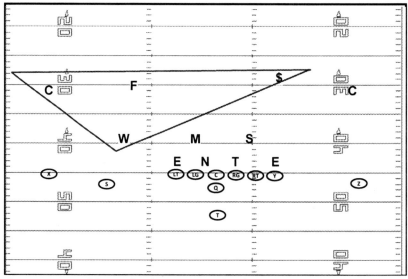

Figure 8-1. Outside receiver's coverage triangle

nearest alley defender and identify his positioning and posture. Once the coverage triangle has been identified, a wide receiver should use the information gathered to identify what coverage the defense is going to play on the next play and how a wide receiver is going to execute his assignment. Once this has been determined, an outside receiver's pre-snap scan is finished and he can get ready to execute his assignment.

Slot Receiver Pre-Snap Scan

A slot receiver's pre-snap scan is very similar to an outside receiver's and uses the same basic principles, with some slight variations. A slot receiver should use his pre-snap scan to identify his coverage triangle. A slot receiver's coverage triangle consists of both safeties on the field and the nearest alley defender (Figure 8-2).

The first step to identifying a slot receiver's coverage triangle is to scan the field and identify the location and positioning of both safeties on the field. For a slot receiver, finding the location of both safeties is more important than for an outside receiver. A slot receiver has to see both safeties and understand what technique and coverage they're going to play. After identifying the safeties, a slot should receiver should then find the nearest alley defender and analyze his positioning and location. Once a slot receiver has identified both safeties and the nearest alley defender, he'll have completed his coverage triangle. It's also recommended for a slot receiver to take a quick look outside of him and see how the corner is playing the outside receiver. Seeing the corner should only be completed once a slot has identified his coverage triangle. After completing all these steps, a slot receiver will have successfully completed his version of the pre-snap scan.

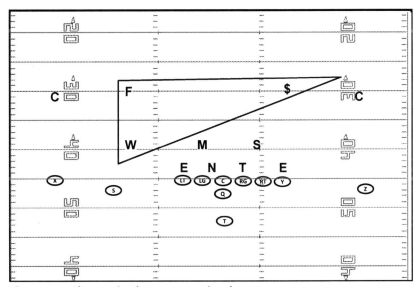

Figure 8-2. Slot receiver's coverage triangle

Seeing the Moving Picture

After a wide receiver performs his pre-snap scan, he should then prepare himself to execute his assignment and see coverage on the run, which is called *seeing the moving picture*. Defenses are always trying to disguise what they're trying to do. They'll show one coverage during the pre-snap scan, then on the snap of the ball, they'll roll to a different coverage. This factor is very important for a wide receiver to understand and to grasp. A wide receiver should use his eyes after the ball is snapped to see what's happening on the field and diagnose what coverage the defense is playing. A wide receiver has to keep his eyes up and see the picture move throughout the play. If a wide receiver can combine the knowledge he's learned about coverage throughout the pre-snap scan with his ability to diagnose coverage on the run, he'll be able ensure he's always adjusting his route to fit the coverage being played.

Coverage Recognition Tips

For a wide receiver to recognize coverage, he should understand what indicators he's looking for to determine what the coverage is. The following sections will give a coverage-by-coverage look at tips and indicators that will help a wide receiver be able to recognize each individual coverage. Each team calls coverages differently throughout football. The following names given to each coverage come from various sources. It doesn't matter what coaches call the coverages; it only matters that each coverage is labeled the same so the entire coaching staff and players all call coverages the same way and speak the same football language.

Cover 4

When playing cover 4, the secondary divides the field into quarters. The four defensive backs on the field are responsible for the deep four quarters of the field. The safeties are aligned usually between 10 and 12 yards off the line of scrimmage and are the primary run support players. The corners are aligned from eight to 10 yards off the line of scrimmage and are the secondary run support players. The underneath coverage is divided into two types of coverage players. The two outside linebackers are curl/flat players, and the Mike linebacker is the hook/curl player. Cover 4 is used by a variety of teams and for all different reasons. It's used by teams wanting to stop the run and also by teams looking for different ways to stop a passing offense due to all its variations. It's a very common coverage seen throughout football (Figure 8-3).

Cover 4 Solo

Cover 4 solo is a cover 4 adjustment that teams will make against 3x1 formations. The corner to the single receiver side will make a solo call, telling the boundary safety he's playing man against the single receiver. The boundary safety will now key the

#3 receiver to the 3x1 side. The Will linebacker will now key the running back and is basically in man coverage with the back if he releases to the boundary of the field. The Mike linebacker will always drop to the three receiver side when playing cover 4 solo (Figure 8-4).

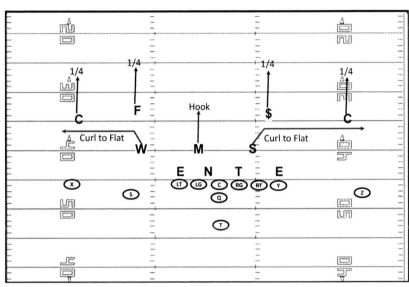

Figure 8-3. Cover 4

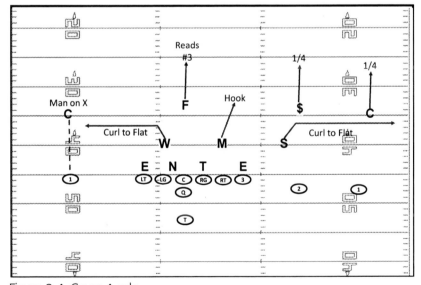

Figure 8-4. Cover 4 solo

Cover 4 Press

Cover 4 press is a variation of cover 4 that teams like to play. The principles of cover 4 press are the same as normal cover 4. The only difference is the corners are playing press man coverage on the outside receivers. If the outside receivers release radically to the inside, the corners will pass the receivers to the curl/flat player and bail into their deep quarter of the field. If the receivers release any other way, the corners will stick with them and play man coverage (Figure 8-5).

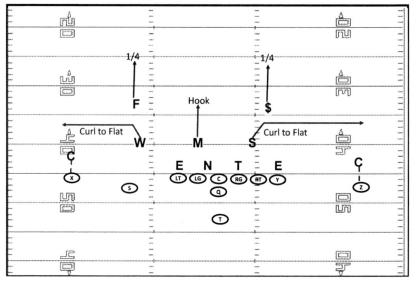

Figure 8-5. Cover 4 press

Cover 4 Mix

Cover 4 mix is another variation of cover 4 that teams play. When playing mix, the corner, safety, and outside linebacker work together. The corner is reading the #2 receiver. If #2 runs a pass route to the flat, then the corner will jump #2 and the safety to his side will work over the top of the #1 receiver (Figure 8-6A). If #2 runs a vertical route, then the corner will shift his eyes to #1 and work to stay on top. Playing mix allows the alley player to the mix side to look to wall #2 on any vertical route and sit in the curl (Figure 8-6B).

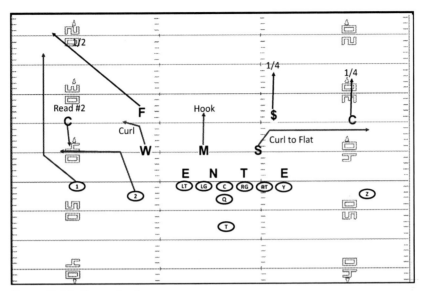

Figure 8-6A. Cover 4 mix

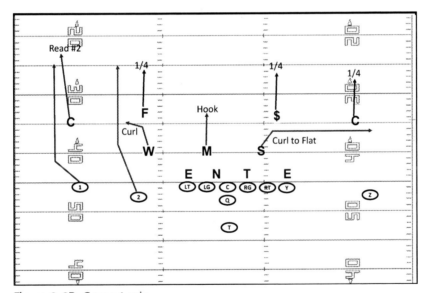

Figure 8-6B. Cover 4 mix

Cover 2

Cover 2 is defined by having two deep half-field safeties and five underneath coverage defenders. The deep half-field safeties usually align between 12 and 15 yards from the line of scrimmage. Their job is to split the difference between the #1 and #2 receivers and keep everything in front of them. The corners in cover 2 are the flat defenders. They try to maintain outside leverage on the #1 receiver and can't let #1 release outside of them. The corners in cover 2 usually align four to five yards off the ball or will press the #1 receiver and settle in the flat. The outside linebackers or alley players are wall defenders in cover 2. They'll work to wall #2, then settle into the curl. The Mike linebacker in normal cover 2 is a low hole player. Cover 2 is used by teams looking to stop pass-oriented offenses (Figure 8-7).

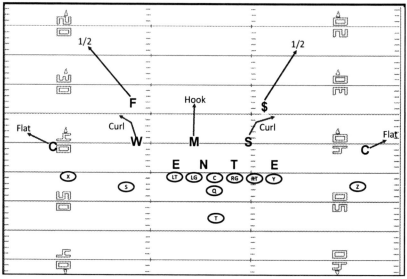

Figure 8-7. Cover 2

Tampa 2

Tampa 2 is a popular variation of cover 2 that teams like to play. Tampa 2 requires the Mike linebacker to open and drop working to take away the high hole or middle of the field. The Mike in Tampa 2 will primarily drop to the field or the 3x1 receiver side. Having the Mike in the middle of the field allows the safeties to work off the hashes more in Tampa 2 and work to take away the pocket between the flat defending corner and the half-field safety. Tampa 2 is a coverage that teams like to play against pass-oriented teams or in long-yardage situations (Figure 8-8).

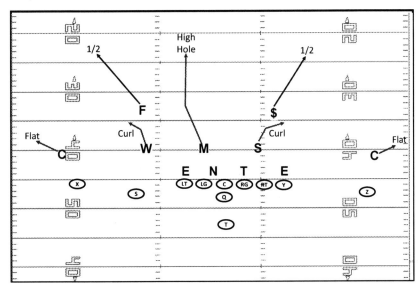

Figure 8-8. Tampa 2

Cover 24

When teams pressure from a two-deep-safety shell, they'll play cover 24. Cover 24 is defined by having two deep half-field safeties and four underneath defenders. The two inside defenders are hook/curl players in cover 24. The corners are flat defenders, and the safeties are half-field players. Cover 24 is used by teams that like to use zone blitzing as a way to pressure the quarterback. Cover 24 gives defenses the advantage of being able to bring pressure but still have two deep defenders protecting against a long pass or a big run (Figure 8-9).

Cover 2 Tilt

When teams want to pressure by blitzing four defenders to one side but still want to play cover 2, they'll run cover 2 tilt. Cover 2 tilt requires the corner away from the pressure side to run to the hash and become a half-field player. The safety away from the pressure will run to the pressure side and become the other half-field player. Two hook/curl defenders will remain in the middle of the defense. The corner to the pressure side will become a flat defender. Away from the pressure, the defense should drop a player to the flat to have a boundary flat defender. Cover 2 tilt and the pressures that come with it are primarily used against 12 personnel formations and groupings (Figure 8-10).

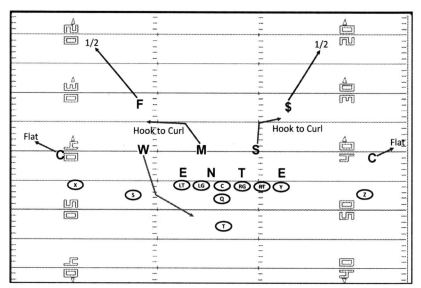

Figure 8-9. Cover 24

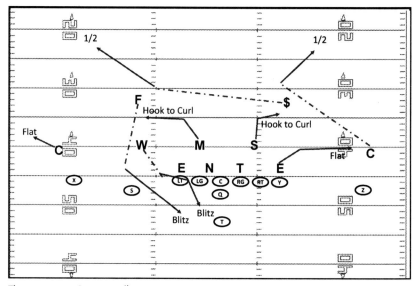

Figure 8-10. Cover 2 tilt

Cover 6 (Combo Coverage)

Cover 6 is a coverage that uses a combination of cover 2 and cover 4. To the field, teams will play cover 4 principles. The safety and corner to the field play deep quarters, and the alley defender is a curl/flat defender. To the boundary, teams play cover 2 principles when playing cover 6. The boundary safety is a half-field player, and the corner is the flat defender. In cover 6, the boundary corner will maintain outside leverage and try to funnel a wide receiver to the half-field safety. In cover 6, the two inside linebackers are hook/curl defenders. Cover 6 gives teams the benefits of using cover 4 and cover 2 (Figure 8-11).

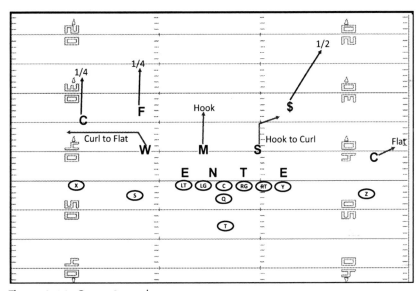

Figure 8-11. Cover 6 combo coverage

Cover 3

The basic premise of cover 3 is for the defense to have three deep defenders who keep everything in front of them. The three deep defenders divide the field into thirds. The middle safety is aligned between 12 and 15 yards deep. The two corners align between eight and 10 yards deep, with inside leverage on the #1 receiver. To get to a three-deep shell, the defense will rotate the other safety down either before or after the snap of the ball. Teams vary on which side the safety will rotate to. Some teams prefer the drop-down safety to rotate to the strength of the formation, while some teams will rotate the safety weak. The primary reason teams play cover 3 is to add an extra defender to the box to help stop the run. Also, cover 3 is a versatile coverage for teams to pressure from (Figure 8-12).

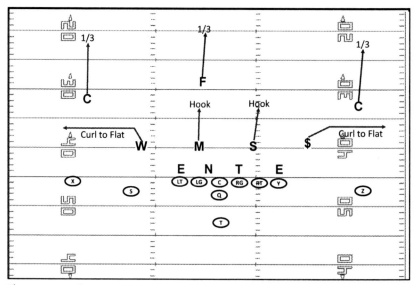

Figure 8-12. Cover 3

Cover 3 Switch

Cover 3 switch has the same basic premise of normal cover 3. The difference is where the drop-down safety rotates to. In cover 3 switch, the drop-down safety will rotate down and become the hook/curl defender to the side he rotates to. Teams that play cover 3 switch like to use the coverage because it's easy to roll into from a two-high-safety shell after the ball is snapped. Teams will start showing a two-high-safety look, then at the snap, the drop-down safety will roll and become the inside hook/curl defender. Like with normal cover 3, teams like to use cover 3 switch to add an extra defender to support the run (Figure 8-13).

Cover 3 Cloud

Cover 3 cloud is a tilted coverage that teams use as a variation to playing normal cover 3. In normal cover 3, covering throws to the flat can be difficult. Cover 3 cloud is used by teams to take away flat throws while still maintaining a three-deep-defender shell. Teams will cloud the side of the formation that teams tend to throw to. To the cloud side, the corner will play outside leverage and sit in the flat. The safety to the cloud side has to get off the hash and play the sideline deep third of the field. The safety away from the cloud has to rotate to the middle third of the field. The corner away from the cloud side is responsible for the final third of the field. Against 3x1 formations, teams that cloud to the strength will lock up the corner to the single receiver side and have him play man coverage on the single receiver (Figure 8-14).

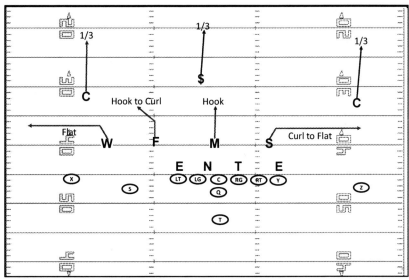

Figure 8-13. Cover 3 switch

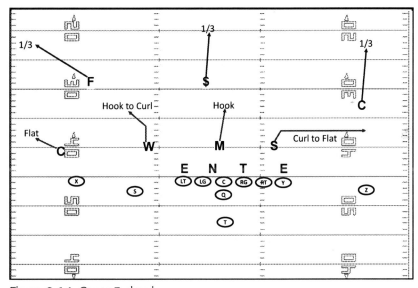

Figure 8-14. Cover 3 cloud

Cover 3 Cloud Boundary

Cover 3 cloud boundary is another variation of cover 3 cloud that teams will play. The same principles are applied whether teams cloud the field or the boundary. The reason teams will play cover 3 cloud boundary is to take away easy throws to the single receiver in 3x1 formations (Figure 8-15).

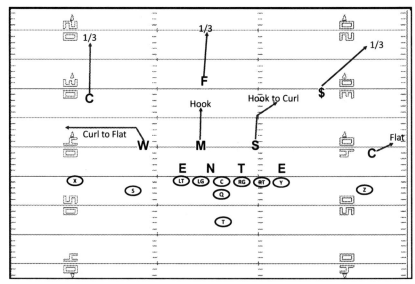

Figure 8-15. Cover 3 cloud boundary

Cover 3 Max Double Cloud

Cover 3 max double cloud is drop-eight coverage. Drop eight means eight defenders drop into coverage and only three defenders rush the quarterback. Cover 3 max double cloud is used in long-yardage situations or against pass-heavy teams. The principles of cover 3 max are actually a lot like Tampa 2. The difference is the high-hole player is aligned pre-snap 10 to 12 yards deep and plays the middle third of the field. Teams will classify this coverage as cover 3 max instead of cover 2 max because of the pre-snap alignment of the middle-third defender (Figure 8-16).

Cover 33 (3 Deep 3 Under)

Cover 33 is zone pressure coverage. Cover 33 can be defined as having three deep defenders playing thirds and three underneath defenders. The three underneath defenders are made up of two skiff players (seam/curl/flat) and one hole player. The skiff player in cover 33 has three coverage responsibilities: He should be able to carry the seam of the field first, then take away any curl throws, and, finally, finish in the flat of the field. The skiff player away from the pressure is usually a dropping defensive end. The hole player is usually a linebacker or defensive tackle that's not involved in the pressure pattern. When running zone pressure coverages, most teams will start off by showing a two-high-safety look. Before the snap, the safeties will rotate toward the side from which pressure is coming. The drop-down safety will become the skiff player toward the pressure side. The other safety will rotate to the middle of the field and play the middle third of the field (Figure 8-17).

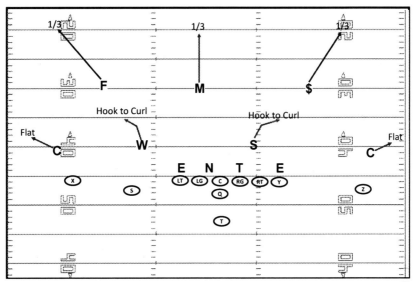

Figure 8-16. Cover 3 max double cloud

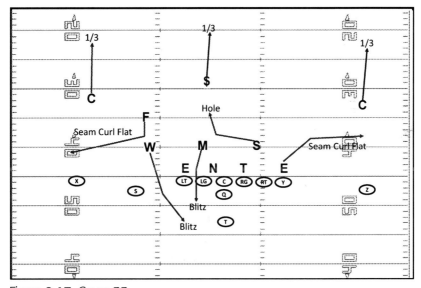

Figure 8-17. Cover 33

Cover 1 Hole

Cover 1 hole is man coverage without bringing pressure. When playing cover 1 hole, the corners will play with inside leverage and their eyes will be locked on their man. The defender playing over the slot will play with outside leverage to funnel the slot to the free safety. The two inside linebackers will combo the running back. Whatever side the running back releases to, the linebacker to that side will cover him. The linebacker away from the side the running back releases from will drop and become the low-hole player. Cover 1 hole is played by teams that like to play man coverage and have the ability to put pressure on the quarterback by rushing only four defenders (Figure 8-18).

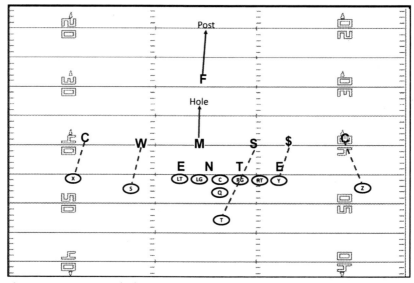

Figure 8-18. Cover 1 hole

Cover 1 No Hole

Teams that bring pressure and play man coverage will play cover 1 without a hole player. When playing cover 1 no hole, the corners will play with inside leverage, and their eyes will be locked on their man. The defender playing over the slot will play with outside leverage to funnel the slot to the free safety. Playing cover 1 while bringing pressure doesn't allow the inside linebackers to combo the running back; instead, each linebacker not involved in the pressure pattern is assigned a man to cover (Figure 8-19).

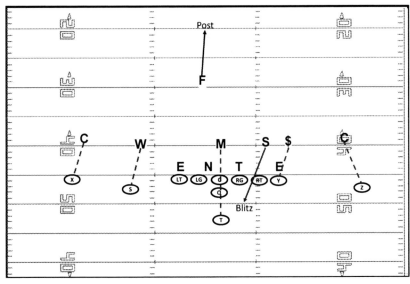

Figure 8-19. Cover 1 no hole

Cover 1 Peel

Cover 1 peel is a version of man coverage that teams will play when they want to pressure with more than one linebacker and still keep a safety in the middle of the field as a deep post player. When playing cover 1 peel, the defensive ends should key the running back as they rush. If the running back releases to the flat, then the defensive end to that side will peel and cover the running back. If the running back releases through the line of scrimmage, then one the blitzing linebackers will peel off and cover the running back. Most teams prefer to pressure and play cover 1 peel when they know the opposing team's running back is part of the protection in to maximize their pass rush (Figure 8-20).

Cover 0

When teams want to maximize the amount of pressure they can put on the quarterback, they'll play cover 0 and pressure with either six or seven defenders. When teams play cover 0, the safeties are the key to recognizing the coverage. When playing cover 0, teams will usually try to disguise the coverage and at the last second will roll the safeties down to be in position to cover. Teams that recognize cover 0 will usually try to get rid of the football quick to avoid the pressure from the pass rush. In cover 0, the corners will either play press coverage on the outside receivers or play off with inside leverage. The safeties can also press but will usually play off with inside leverage (Figure 8-21).

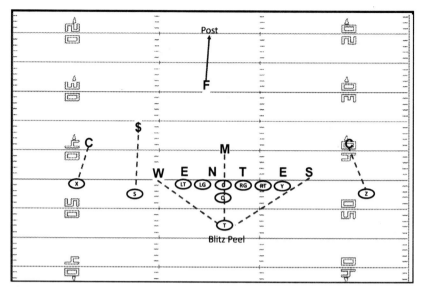

Figure 8-20. Cover 1 peel

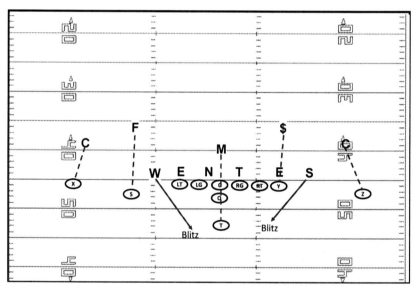

Figure 8-21. Cover 0

Cover 2 Man

Cover 2 man is a mix of cover 2 and man coverage. Teams that play cover 2 man will usually press all the receivers across the field. The pressed defenders use a hard physical press technique at the line of scrimmage. In cover 2 man, the pressed defenders can afford to be more physical at the line of scrimmage because they have safety help over the top from the half-field safeties. Once the receivers release off the line of scrimmage, the defenders will play in a trail technique. The defenders over the slots will play with outside leverage and work to get to a trail position to take away the underneath throw. The corners will play with inside leverage and also work to get to a trail position. Teams tend to play cover 2 man in long-yardage or passing situations (Figure 8-22).

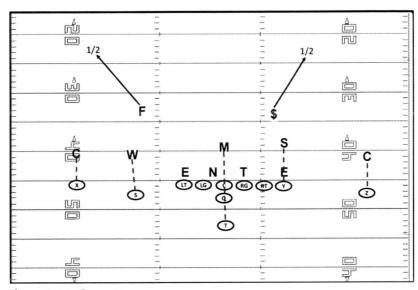

Figure 8-22. Cover 2 man

About the Author

Matt Troxel is the inside receiver coach and special teams coordinator at Idaho State University, where he has helped the Bengals become one of the finest passing offenses in the country, finishing ninth nationally in passing in 2011 and fourth nationally in 2012. He coached tight end Josh Hill to All–Big Sky Conference honors in 2011 and 2012. Hill also led the nation in catches for a tight end with 70 in 2012.

Matt is a 2009 graduate of the University of Montana, with a degree in history, political science, and secondary education. Matt was a three-year letter winner for the Grizzlies as a wide receiver, kick returner, and punt returner. While at Montana, Matt was a part of the Grizzlies' Big Sky championship teams from 2004 to 2007. The 2004 team was also the FCS national runner-up, and the 2006 team made it to the FCS semifinals. Recurring injuries cut short Matt's playing career but landed him in a role as the student assistant wide receivers coach in 2008. While at Montana, Matt coached current Tennessee Titans wide receiver Marc Mariani, who was a fifth-round NFL draft pick. The 2008 Grizzlies would once again win the Big Sky Championship and finish as the FCS runner-up with a record of 14-2.

After the 2008 season, Matt left to work as a graduate assistant at the University of Idaho. Matt would spend the 2009 season working with the Vandals' wide receivers, most notably Max Komar, who was named Second-Team All-Western Athletic Conference and signed as a free agent with the Arizona Cardinals after the 2009 season. The 2009 Vandals went on to win the Humanitarian Bowl and finish ranked ninth nationally in total offense. In 2010, Matt worked with the Vandals' offense line. The 2010 Vandals offense would finish ranked 10th nationally in passing. Matt received his master's degree in physical education from the University of Idaho in 2010.

Matt is from a football coaching family. Matt's father, Van Troxel, is a longtime high school coach in the state of Idaho and played quarterback at the University of Montana. Van is currently the coach at Lake City High School in Coeur d'Alene. Matt's grandfather, Ed Troxel, was the head coach at the University of Idaho from 1973 to 1976 and a coaching legend in the state of Idaho and Washington as the head coach of Borah High School in Boise, Idaho, and Kennewick High School in Kennewick, Washington. Matt's other grandfather, Joe Roberts, was a longtime high school coach in Butte, Montana, and Missoula, Montana.

Matt and his wife, Katie, currently reside in Pocatello, Idaho.